venturesome
VEGAN COOKING

Copyright © 2004 by J.M. Hirsch and Michelle Hirsch.

Printed in China.

Venturesome Vegan Cooking: Bold Flavors For Plant-Based Meals
ISBN-10: 1-57284-114-1
ISBN-13: 978-1-57284-114-7

Design by Brandtner Design
Photography by Larry Crowe

Originally published as *Venturesome Vegetarian Cooking: Bold Flavors for Meat- and Dairy-free Meals*

The Library of Congress has cataloged the previous edition of this book as follows:

Library of Congress Cataloging-in-Publication Data:
Hirsch, J.M.
    Venturesome vegetarian cooking: bold flavors for meat- and dairy-free meals / J.M. Hirsch and Michelle
    Hirsch. —1st ed.
    p. cm.
    ISBN 1-57284-064-1
    1. Vegetarian cookery. 2. Cookery, International. I. Hirsch, Michelle. II. Title.
    TX837.H58 2004
    641.5'636—dc22

                                         2003024885

14 13 12 11 10   5 4 3 2 1

Surrey Books is an imprint of Agate Publishing, Inc.
Agate and Surrey books are available in bulk at discount prices. For more information, go to agatepublishing.com.

venturesome
VEGAN COOKING
bold flavors for plant-based meals

J.M. HIRSCH AND MICHELLE HIRSCH

PHOTOGRAPHY BY LARRY CROWE

Surrey Books, Chicago

contents

foreword

MY SWITCH TO A PLANT-BASED DIET came after nearly a quarter century as a sometimes vegetarian who occasionally indulged in seafood, eggs and dairy. Despite the lure of those foods the change was easy, for I found myself unable to refute simple, compelling arguments in favor of a vegan diet, including:

- Eating animals and animal products causes pain and suffering to those creatures.

- Eating animals is unnecessary for good health. In fact, those who build their diets around whole foods and eat the fewest animal products often enjoy the best personal health, well-being and longevity.

- The pleasure of my palate is insufficient reason to cause animals pain.

Becoming vegan was the most ethical choice. I want a life of compassion for all beings, not exploitation. Studies repeatedly have demonstrated that diets high in animal products are bad not only for our bodies but also our environment. The use and abuse of animals diminishes biodiversity, depletes precious resources and creates massive waste disposal and pollution problems.

Since switching to a plant-based diet I feel better, my daily decisions benefit countless creatures and the environment is a safer place.

When I founded Whole Foods Market in 1980, society's understanding of the importance of eating a local, seasonal and organic plant-based diet was in its infancy. But thanks to a corps of committed, concerned people, including company team members, chefs and customers, my vision for the industry blossomed from radical notions into a movement that slowly became a respected and mainstream way of life.

Whole Foods is so much more than a company or a name. It is a philosophy, a way of approaching life that respects the many spheres in which we travel. Our choices matter deeply and affect widely. More than ever, that is true of our food choices.

When we opt for local, organic products, we voice our belief in small community-based farms that respect their lands and the people they feed. I began my company with a vision of Whole People, Whole Planet and Whole Foods and continue to support organic farming and sustainable agricultural practices.

Living and eating respectfully doesn't resign one to a dull diet. As this book demonstrates, it is quite the opposite. Michelle and J.M. illustrate the principles I've emphasized for more than 25 years, showing you how to bring them to the table in a celebration of wellness and good taste.

My focus is on foods free of artificial flavors, colors, sweeteners and preservatives. Research the data, ask questions about the origins of your food and take the time to make informed choices. As these recipes demonstrate, you'll find that a diet of whole foods not only is healthy but also can be as daring and lush as any you'll find.

John Mackey, President and CEO
Whole Foods Market

acknowledgments

SO MANY PEOPLE TO THANK FOR SO MUCH— Mom, for seeing this project through, raising me right and setting the best example for so many years; Dad for encouraging us both, teaching me the pleasure of eating and being a friend as well as a father; Susan Schwartz, a gifted and gracious publisher who convinced us to finally pull this project together; Joan Brunskill, The Associated Press' food editor, for taking me under her wing, taking a risk and trusting me so much; Larry Crowe, food photographer extraordinaire, the essential and satirical other half of a Monty Python-esque partnership; Jon Landry, who saw this coming back in high school and has been my best sounding board ever since; Annmarie Timmins, whose ample generosity of time and energy saved us on deadline; my mother-in-law, Sharon Ramer, who took on the tedious task of copyediting this beast; and our army of testers—Lori and David Ayotte, Scott and Amy Blanchard, Francine Hirsch, Norma Love, Ann Kim, Connie and Whit Miller, Christina Pirello, Charlie Putnam and family, Jeff and Hilary Warner and Katharine Webster.

Even with everyone above, this never could have happened without the love and support of my wife, Holly, who tirelessly edited draft after draft and tasted more tofu than she cares to remember.

J.M. Hirsch

THIS BOOK IS THE RESULT OF THE COORDINATED EFFORTS of many people in various areas of my life. Without their efforts this book would not be.

Michio Kushi and the instructors at the Kushi Institute. From them I learned the importance of food and its relation to health. To them I am forever grateful. Michio has been one of the most influential people in my life.

Carol Bedrosian, the editor and publisher of *Spirit of Change* magazine, for her support and belief in the value of a cooking column devoted to healthy eating, and for the spirit and energy she brings to her wonderful publication.

Whole Foods Market for providing a wealth of organic and healthy products in an environment committed to whole people, whole foods and a whole planet, and for living up to those values in everyday decisions.

To the many people who have dined at my home and sampled the dishes tested for this book. They valiantly ate the "losers" as well as the "keepers" and offered suggestions for improvement.

To my son and co-author, who spent endless hours rewriting recipes and forcing me to conform to a consistent style. Thankfully, we share a love of cooking and, having survived the first book, are talking about the next.

To my husband for his patience, understanding and support for the demands of a project like this and for offering his suggestions on the dishes that made it and those that are best forgotten.

Michelle Hirsch

introduction

FOR MY MÉMÈRE, COOKING WAS A SIMPLE EQUATION—"One for the pot and one for the pot." It was a gastronomic formula that sent a morsel into her potbelly for every one that made it into the pot on the stove.

Though no gourmet, my great-grandmother made simple, satisfying fare that reached back to her French-Canadian roots. Pork scrap was my favorite. The liverwurst-like pâté was rich and delicious spread thick on bread and doused with ketchup. And her turkey soup was heaven. Even after the rest of us had stopped eating meat, she still insisted my father roast a turkey every week so she could have the bones for her broth.

Her habit of feeding both pots probably began as a survival skill. She was one of five children in a family that struggled with meager means and hard jobs in the Massachusetts mills that powered the Industrial Revolution.

By the time I came around some 70 years later, she had matured into a comfortable, portly woman who bustled around our kitchen, occasionally cursing at my father in French and doting on my mother and me. And she still loved to feed the pots.

It's a habit the whole family adopted. I adored my mother's fruit salad as a child, but few apple wedges and banana rounds made it to the bowl if I was nearby. And to this day making sushi is a task if Dad is within reach of the fixings.

But unlike mémère, we weren't poor immigrants scraping by. In fact, when it came to food, we clearly were a little too well off. By the time I was a teenager, we started making changes. We still fed our pots with gusto, but with different morsels.

A vegetarian of many years, Mom led the way, gradually eliminating meat and other animal products from our diets. As our habits changed we learned to replace what we missed with foods that stood on their own merit, not mush that pretended to taste like something it wasn't. It wasn't about replicating; it was about replacing.

Too many people think vegetarian food is dull, that it is rice and broccoli day after day. Maybe for some, but our pots demand more. The world of food is vast and populated by so many flavors that boredom is inexcusable.

We love pizza. Now we eat it without cheese. Instead, breaded eggplant and marinated artichoke hearts decorate our pies. And though I no longer eat mémère's pork scrap, I devour an equally rich hummus that blends the creaminess of cashew butter and chickpeas with the heat of hot peppers.

Eating shouldn't be a hassle, and it shouldn't leave us feeling deprived. Choosing to be vegetarian doesn't mean giving up any of the pleasure of eating and sharing food.

Meals are celebrations of our families, our cultures and the people and places that excite us. Cookbooks are scrapbooks of those celebrations. They collect bits and pieces from the adventures and mishaps that shape who we are and what we value. Writing this book has been an exploration not only of the foods we enjoy but also of how our values and understanding of food, family and community have changed.

Sound a bit deep for a cookbook? Look at your own bookshelves. Dig out the *Betty Crocker* from which your mother baked your first birthday cake, or the first cookbook you bought with your partner. Flip through the recipes and think about the meals you've had, and those you have yet to plan. They are much of who you are.

Mémère isn't with us any more, but she lives on at our table. Over the years we've assembled a broad collection of recipes that represent our family's culinary history, drawn from our memories, our travels, our jobs and our friends. These are not vegetarian recipes that try to taste good. Where is the pleasure in that? These are good recipes that just happen to be vegetarian.

So, from our pots to yours, enjoy.

J.M. Hirsch

authors' note

EVERYONE NEEDS A FAVORITE FARM STAND, the sort of place where the seasons are telegraphed by produce stacked high in wooden bins—melons and eggplant in July, corn and tomatoes in August and apples, pears and pumpkins in September.

Our favorite is Abenaki Spring Farm, a ramshackle place an hour from nowhere in Walpole, N.H. At this organic farm, fresh tastes mesh splendidly with a philosophy of caring for the environment and the consumer; it's well worth the trek.

Drive down the long, winding dirt road to Abenaki Spring and you will see farmer James Johnson grab his pitchfork and a fistful of recycled grocery bags. Ask what's in season and he will rattle off the week's finest. Then place your order and follow him as he heads into the fields and pulls your produce fresh from the earth and vine. Bits of warm soil still cling to it when you get home.

This is food at its finest—local, seasonal and organic. Buy food with those qualities and you never will be disappointed with the meals you make.

There are countless reasons for eating a plant-based diet (or simply more plant-based meals), from concern for the environment and animal welfare to better health and weight loss. Your reasons are your own, so we offer only a few simple principles to ensure your dishes are delicious, no matter what your reasons for making them.

- Whenever possible, choose organic. The nation's top chefs swear by organic for one simple reason—taste.

- For the same reason, eat seasonally and locally. December tomatoes shipped from afar just don't taste as they should. Stick with what's fresh.

- Don't fear convenience foods. If you have time to soak and bake beans from scratch, go for it. But better to crack a can than avoid home cooking entirely.

- Don't let convenience clutter otherwise healthy choices. Pay attention to what you eat; vegetarian junk food is still junk food.

- Eat broadly. This ensures you get a full array of nutrients and keeps your meals interesting. Challenge your palate with new tastes.

- Eat boldly. Don't fear brash, unusual or foreign flavors, even those that don't appear complementary. Need proof? Dunk chocolate in balsamic vinegar.

As much as possible, our recipes are naturally vegetarian. Most do not attempt to mimic meat dishes, though a few rely on soy or seitan in place of animal products.

starters,
pâtés and
spreads

START TO FINISH:

5 minutes

Makes about 2 cups

TIP: Quality olives are essential to tapenade. Canned black olives will suffice in a pinch, but they lack the bold flavor of Kalamata. If you have trouble finding pitted olives, buy a cherry pitter—it works wonderfully.

tapenade

Few foods match the comfort and rich pleasure of tapenade, especially when slathered on a thick slice of baguette and topped with fresh thyme and tomato.

At its heart, tapenade is a paste of olives and olive oil. Traditional versions use anchovies for a bit of zing. Capers do just as well in this recipe.

6 ounces (about 40) pitted Kalamata olives

6 ounces (about 40) pitted Spanish olives

2 tablespoons drained capers

2 tablespoons extra-virgin olive oil

1 teaspoon fresh lemon juice

1 tablespoon fresh oregano leaves

1 tablespoon fresh thyme leaves

1 teaspoon balsamic vinegar

2 cloves garlic, peeled

Place all ingredients in the bowl of a food processor and pulse until a coarse, thick mixture is formed. Transfer to a bowl and serve immediately or chill 1 hour.

To store tapenade in the refrigerator, cover top with a thin layer of olive oil. Mix thoroughly before serving.

artichoke tapenade

Here's a twist on tapenade, which traditionally calls for olives puréed with either anchovies or capers and drizzled with olive oil. This version retains the olive oil and capers but replaces the tangy tartness of olives with creamy artichokes and roasted garlic. Eat this with crackers, bread or as a dip for fresh vegetables.

START TO FINISH:
1½ hours
(25 minutes active)
Makes about 1½ cups

TIP: For a deeper, richer flavor, add 1 tablespoon Dijon mustard when ready to purée. For a creamier version, add 2 tablespoons soy mayonnaise.

2 medium heads garlic

⅓ cup extra-virgin olive oil

14-ounce can artichoke hearts, drained

1 cup sweet white wine (inexpensive Rieslings work well)

⅓ cup cider vinegar

½ teaspoon freshly ground black pepper

2 tablespoons drained capers

Preheat the oven to 400°F.

Set each garlic head on its side and slice off the upper tip, exposing the tops of the cloves. Peel away and discard any papery skin. Place each head on a square of foil about 10 × 10 inches.

Drizzle 1 tablespoon of oil over each bulb and loosely wrap the foil around the garlic. Bake 30 minutes. Uncover and bake an additional 15 minutes or until the garlic is soft. Remove from the oven, unwrap and cool 5 minutes.

While the garlic cooks, place the artichokes in a medium saucepan along with the wine and cider vinegar. Simmer over a medium-high flame until nearly all the liquid has reduced, about 15 minutes.

Transfer the artichokes, any remaining liquid and all remaining ingredients to a food processor.

One at a time, grip each garlic head by its base and squeeze the cloves into the food processor. Discard the skins.

Process the ingredients until chunky smooth.

spicy creamy hummus

START TO FINISH:

5 minutes

Makes about 2 cups

TIP: For a tasty twist, lightly sauté the chickpeas in olive oil and a teaspoon of curry powder before proceeding with the recipe.

Try mixing in chopped green olives after the hummus is puréed.

Most hummus combines chickpeas with tahini for a creamy texture. But tahini can be bitter. Roasted tahini, rather than the more common raw, is better but not great.

This recipe replaces tahini with cashew nut butter, which is creamier. Because we like our hummus with a bit of zing, we also add vinegar and hot pepper sauce. We find the vinegar highlights the subtle flavors of the chickpeas and olive oil.

We like to serve this with a stack of fresh hot flatbread (recipe p. 29). It also is great with tortilla chips or crunchy crostini.

15-ounce can chickpeas (liquid reserved)

¾ **cup cashew butter**

Juice of 1 lemon

½ **teaspoon sea salt**

¼ **cup extra-virgin olive oil**

2 **tablespoons red wine vinegar or balsamic vinegar**

1 **tablespoon hot pepper sauce**

Paprika, for garnish (optional)

Combine all ingredients in a food processor and purée until smooth. Add reserved chickpea liquid as needed to reach desired consistency.

Transfer hummus to a small bowl and sprinkle with paprika, if using.

sweet potato aioli

Try this rich spread as a dip with crackers or flatbread, or use it as a sandwich spread with tomatoes and greens. The almonds lend nutty undertones to the creaminess of the sweet potatoes.

2 large sweet potatoes

¾ cup whole raw almonds

5 cloves garlic

2 tablespoons lemon juice

¼ cup extra-virgin olive oil

1 teaspoon paprika

1 teaspoon ground cumin

½ teaspoon sea salt

¼ teaspoon freshly ground black pepper

Bring 2 inches of water to a boil in a medium saucepan fitted with a steamer basket. While the water boils, peel the sweet potatoes, then cut them into 1-inch chunks.

Steam the potatoes, covered, 10–12 minutes or until soft and easily pierced with a fork. Remove from the heat and set aside to cool.

While the sweet potatoes cool, heat a large, heavy skillet over a medium-high flame. Add the almonds and toast, stirring frequently, until fragrant, about 5 minutes.

Combine all ingredients in a food processor and pulse until chunky smooth. Serve at room temperature or slightly chilled.

START TO FINISH:
25 minutes
Makes about 2 ½ cups

TIP: Bake the sweet potatoes ahead of time, then cover them in plastic wrap and refrigerate up to 2 days before using. The sweet potatoes will have a smoother texture if allowed to come to room temperature before blending.

Save time by purchasing toasted, unsalted almonds.

tomato crostini

Crostini are an Italian staple and a great way to start a meal. These toasted rounds of bread can carry any number of ingredients, but we like this simple and tangy tomato topping best. Size, not toppings, differentiates crostini from bruschetta. Crostini are small (a baguette sliced into rounds), while bruschetta are larger (usually a full slice from a rustic loaf).

START TO FINISH:

15 minutes
Makes 12 breadsticks

TIP: For a cheesy version, sprinkle with shredded soy mozzarella cheese during the final few minutes of baking.

- 4 large tomatoes
- 2 teaspoons sea salt or kosher salt
- ½ teaspoon freshly ground black pepper
- 1 teaspoon dried oregano
- 1 teaspoon dried basil
- 2 tablespoons balsamic vinegar
- 12-inch baguette or French bread
- Extra-virgin olive oil
- Fresh basil leaves, as garnish (whole or cut into ribbons)

Preheat the oven to 400°F. Dice the tomatoes and transfer to a medium bowl.

Add the salt, pepper, oregano, basil and vinegar to the tomatoes and mix well with a wooden spoon or your hands. Transfer the tomatoes to a mesh strainer and set over a bowl or sink. Drain 12–15 minutes.

Meanwhile, slice the bread into ¼- to ½-inch thick rounds. Lightly coat a large baking sheet with olive oil.

Arrange the rounds on the baking sheet. Drizzle a few drops of additional olive oil over each round. Bake until lightly toasted, about 5 minutes.

Allow the rounds to cool 5 minutes, then arrange on a serving platter.

Top each round with roughly 1 tablespoon of tomato mixture, and drizzle with additional olive oil. Top with a fresh basil leaf.

crostini di fave (crostini with fava bean pâté)

START TO FINISH:

20 minutes

Makes 2 cups

TIP: To make this dish from dried beans, start with 1½ cups of dry fava beans. Soak the beans in a large pot of water 12 hours. Drain and add 6 cups fresh water, 1 diced carrot, ½ cup diced onion and 1 stick celery, chopped.

Bring the beans to a boil, cover and simmer 1½ hours or until tender. Drain the beans, then peel off and discard the skins.

We discovered this gem of an appetizer while dining with friends at a charming tratoria called Bacco Felice in Foligno, Italy. Salvatore Denaro, the charismatic owner of the combination wine cellar, cheese shop and restaurant, offered no menus and no English. He simply presented course after course of magnificent dishes that melted language barriers.

This beguilingly elegant appetizer of olive oil-drizzled toasts smeared with a fava bean hummus packs plenty of flavor in a simple package.

Salvatore probably never would dream of using canned beans, and he likes to use ham fat instead of olive oil. We admit the taste of fresh beans is superior, but since few of us have the time and patience required, we've adapted this for canned beans and vegetarian sensibilities.

Should you have the time to use dry beans, see TIP, then proceed to the remainder of the recipe.

> **12-inch baguette**
> ¼ **cup extra-virgin olive oil, plus 1 tablespoon**
> 2 **cups cooked *or* canned fava beans**
> ½ **teaspoon sea salt**
> ¼ **cup vegetable broth**

Preheat the oven to 350°F. Slice the bread into thin rounds, about ¼ inch thick.

Lightly oil a baking sheet with ⅛ cup oil. Arrange the bread slices on the sheet. Drizzle another ⅛ cup oil over the bread. Bake until lightly toasted, about 5 minutes.

Meanwhile, use a food processor to purée all but ⅓ cup of the fava beans. Add the remaining beans and pulse 5–10 seconds to chop but not purée.

In a large skillet, combine bean mixture, remaining oil, salt and broth. Heat over a medium flame 5 minutes, stirring frequently.

Top each round of bread with the pâté and arrange on a serving platter.

veggie ribbons

For a crispier version, combine raw veggie ribbons in a plastic bag with the seasonings, seal and shake. Arrange the vegetables on a baking sheet, salt lightly and bake at 350°F 15 minutes or until just browned and crisp.

3 large carrots

4 small zucchini

4 small yellow summer squash

2 teaspoons extra-virgin olive oil

2 cloves garlic, minced

2 teaspoons balsamic vinegar

1 tablespoon chopped fresh parsley

1 teaspoon dried thyme

Pinch sea salt

Shave the carrots, zucchini and squash into long ribbons using a vegetable peeler. Alternatively, cut the vegetables with a knife into long matchsticks.

Heat the oil in a deep skillet over a medium flame. Add the garlic and cook 1 minute. Add carrots and cook another minute. Add the zucchini and squash and cook 4 minutes or until the vegetables are just tender.

Stir in the vinegar, parsley, thyme and salt, and cook 1 minute. Serve immediately as is or drizzle with additional balsamic vinegar and extravirgin olive oil.

START TO FINISH:

20 minutes

Makes 4–6 servings

TIP: Many companies now make vegetable peelers that cut produce into long, thin ribbons that are perfect for this recipe

derbs

These simple yet delicious breadsticks are great as is, dipped in hummus or cut into croutons for a salad. The name—a bastardization of hors d'oeuvres—is borrowed from a lowbrow version made by a friend's mother.

1	medium loaf French bread
½	cup soy margarine
1	teaspoon minced fresh rosemary
3–4	cloves garlic, finely minced
2	teaspoons finely minced onion *or* 1 teaspoon onion powder
½	teaspoon sea salt

Preheat the oven to 425°F.

Cut bread in half lengthwise, as though making a large sandwich. Cut each half into 6 pieces.

In a small bowl, combine remaining ingredients. Spread the mixture on the cut sides of the breadsticks.

Arrange the breadsticks on a baking sheet. Bake 7–9 minutes or until lightly toasted.

START TO FINISH:

15 minutes
Makes 12 breadsticks

TIP: For a cheesy version, sprinkle with shredded soy mozzarella cheese during the final few minutes of baking.

scallion pancakes

We had a version of these at our favorite Vietnamese restaurant and loved them so much we had to make them at home.

2 cups unbleached white flour

1 cup boiling water

1 tablespoon toasted sesame seed oil

3 tablespoons extra-virgin olive oil

½ cup diced scallions

Sea salt and freshly ground black pepper, to taste

Place the flour in the bowl of a food processor. Start the processor and slowly add the water through the feed tube. Continue adding water until the dough forms a ball. Remove the dough from the processor and cover with a damp cloth. Let rest 30 minutes. The flour and water also can be mixed by hand in a large bowl, adding the water gradually while stirring.

Lightly flour a smooth surface and roll out the dough into a thin rectangle, about ¼ inch thick and measuring roughly 12 × 9 inches. In a small dish, mix together the sesame and olive oils. Brush the surface of the dough with the oil mixture. Sprinkle the dough evenly with the scallions, salt and pepper.

Roll up the dough into a log and cut into 4 equal pieces. Form each piece into a ball, being careful not to spill the ingredients inside.

Using a rolling pin, roll each piece of dough into a 6-inch-round pancake. Lightly coat a hot, cast-iron skillet with extra-virgin olive oil. Cook each pancake until lightly browned on both sides, about 3 minutes per side.

Cut each pancake into 4 wedges and serve immediately.

START TO FINISH:
1 hour
(15 minutes active)
Makes 2–4 servings

TIP: Don't trim the green ends off scallions; it wastes the best part. Use a sharp knife to slice off only the very tips of each stalk, then dice the entire scallion.

For a quick dipping sauce, combine 3 tablespoons each of tamari, brown rice vinegar and chopped scallions. Add ½ teaspoon each of grated fresh ginger and red pepper flakes, along with 3 teaspoons brown rice syrup or sugar. Whisk together or combine in a jar and shake vigorously.

luscious latkes

Potato pancakes are great hot and crispy from the oven and dipped in warm Pesto Tomato Sauce. Or try them cold the next day with a bit of ketchup.

START TO FINISH:

1 hour

Makes 6–8 latkes

TIP: Liven up these latkes by adding a little hot pepper sauce to the batter. Or dust them with paprika just before baking.

LATKES

3	medium potatoes, peeled and quartered
¼	cup nutritional yeast flakes
1¼	teaspoons sea salt
½	teaspoon freshly ground black pepper
1	cup grated carrot (about 2 carrots)
½	cup corn kernels
2	tablespoons extra-virgin olive oil
¼	cup soft, silken tofu
1	cup matzo meal

PESTO TOMATO SAUCE

¼	cup pine nuts
2	tablespoons extra-virgin olive oil
½	cup fresh basil leaves
1	tablespoon nutritional yeast flakes
3	large tomatoes, diced, seeds and juice retained
1½	tablespoons red wine vinegar
½	teaspoon sea salt
½	teaspoon freshly ground black pepper

Bring a medium saucepan of water to a boil. Add the potatoes and cook until tender, about 20 minutes.

Drain the potatoes and run under cold water 30 seconds. Drip-dry potatoes 2 minutes, then transfer to a large mixing bowl.

Preheat the oven to 350°F.

Mash the potatoes. Add the ¼ cup yeast flakes, salt, pepper, carrots and corn, one ingredient at a time, stirring between each addition.

Combine 2 tablespoons olive oil and the tofu in a blender and purée until smooth. Add to the potato mixture and mix well.

Add the matzo and mix until the mixture is sticky but still fairly dry.

Lightly coat a baking sheet with additional olive oil. Form ½-inch-thick patties about the size of hamburgers. Arrange the patties on the baking sheet, leaving 1 inch between each patty.

Bake the patties 20 minutes or until the tops begin to brown. Flip the patties with a spatula and bake another 20 minutes.

Meanwhile, make the sauce by lightly toasting the pine nuts in a dry skillet over a medium-high flame until just lightly browned, about 4 minutes.

Transfer the nuts to a food processor or blender and add 2 tablespoons olive oil, basil and 1 tablespoon yeast flakes. Process until mostly smooth, leaving some texture.

Combine the tomatoes, with seeds and juices, vinegar, salt and pepper in a small saucepan and bring to a simmer. Cook 4 minutes.

Stir in the nut and basil mixture. Simmer another 2 minutes.

To serve, ladle several tablespoons of sauce over each patty.

fresh spring rolls

These fresh spring rolls are packed with a variety of crisp vegetables. Strips of roasted red pepper also make a good filling. Set out the ingredients and let your guests make their own.

START TO FINISH:

30 minutes

Makes 12 rolls

TIP: Don't soak the rice-paper wrappers too long or they will fall apart. The wrappers soften quickly, so do one at a time. Most natural food stores and Asian markets offer a variety of sizes. A large cake pan makes an excellent soaking bowl.

2 ounces dried bean thread noodles or rice thread noodles

1 cucumber, peeled and cut in half lengthwise

12 large rice-paper wrappers (8-inch round or larger)

2 cups baby spinach leaves (or other hardy greens such as kale or Romaine lettuce), cut in thin strips

1 medium carrot, cut into matchsticks

8 ounces baked, seasoned tofu, cut into ¼-inch sticks

12 fresh basil or mint leaves

Peanut Sauce (recipe p. 156)

Place the noodles in a bowl and cover with hot water. Soak 5 minutes or until softened. Drain well in a mesh strainer and set aside.

Cut each cucumber length in half crosswise. Remove and discard the seeds by scraping a spoon down the center of each piece. Cut each piece into thin strips.

Fill a large bowl (at least several inches larger than the rice wrappers) with warm water. Soak 1 wrapper in the water until soft and pliable, 20–30 seconds.

Remove the rice wrapper from the water and lay flat on a counter or cutting board. Place 1–2 tablespoons of spinach leaves along one edge of the wrapper. Place an equal amount of noodles over the spinach.

Top the spinach with 1–2 tablespoons of carrots and several pieces each of cucumber and tofu. Top the ingredients with a basil or mint leaf.

Roll the wrapper, starting with the filling side, folding the ends over the filling as you roll and forming a tight cylinder.

Serve with small bowls of Peanut Sauce for dipping.

california sushi rolls

We are sushi addicts. We'll eat just about anything you care to wrap in rice and nori (tempura-fried sweet potato is particularly popular), but California rolls are among our favorites.

FOR THE RICE:

1	**cup white sushi rice**
1⅓	**cups water**
¼	**cup seasoned rice vinegar**

Place the rice in a mesh strainer and rinse under cold water until it runs clear. Leave the rice in the strainer and drain 1 hour.

Transfer the rice to a small saucepan. Add the water and bring to a boil over a medium-high flame. Cover and reduce the heat to low. Simmer 14 minutes without removing the cover.

Remove the pan from the heat and uncover. Drape a dish towel over the pan, then replace the cover. Let the rice stand 20 minutes. This step is important for achieving the proper moisture content for the rice.

Transfer the rice to a shallow dish and add the vinegar. Use a wooden spoon to toss the rice with the vinegar until well mixed. Make sushi while rice is still slightly warm.

FOR THE SUSHI ROLL:

2	**tablespoons sesame seeds**
4	**sheets nori seaweed**
	Wasabi paste
1	**carrot, cut into thin matchsticks**
1	**small cucumber (about 4 inches), peeled, seeded and cut into thin strips**
4	**ounces baked, seasoned tofu, cut into thin strips similar to the cucumber**
1	**avocado, peeled, pitted and cut into thin strips**

Place the sesame seeds in a dry skillet and cook over a medium flame 3–4 minutes or until seeds are just lightly browned. Set aside.

Place a sheet of nori seaweed, shiny side down, on a bamboo mat or smooth cutting board. Dip both hands in a bowl of water.

START TO FINISH:
2 hours
(25 minutes active)
Makes 4 rolls (or 24 pieces), appetizers for 4–6, or a main course for 2

TIP: One of the hardest parts of preparing good sushi at home is cooking the rice. We use a recipe perfected by the least likely of sushi chefs— Dad (a Jewish electrical engineer). It works without fail. Be sure to use sushi rice for this recipe. Short-grain brown rice can be used, but it won't taste quite the same as restaurant sushi.

Other good sushi fillings include sliced Portobello mushrooms, strips of roasted red pepper, steamed kale, refried beans and roasted or steamed sweet potatoes.

For something different, replace the wasabi inside the roll with peanut butter and the fillings with strips of seasoned, cooked tempeh.

Using your fingers, spread about ¼ of the rice evenly over the nori, leaving a ¾-inch strip bare along the far edge.

Spread a pinch of wasabi across the center of the rice. Sprinkle the rice with sesame seeds, then arrange several strips each of carrot, cucumber, tofu and avocado along the line of wasabi. The fillings should extend to both sides of the nori.

Use your index fingers and thumbs to pick up the edge of the bamboo mat (if not using a mat, grasp the nori) closest to you. Place your remaining fingers over the fillings to hold them in place. Roll forward, tightly wrapping the rice and nori around the fillings.

Roll until you reach the ¾-inch strip of bare nori. Lightly wet several fingers with water and run them across the uncovered nori. Continue rolling, pressing the moistened strip of nori against the roll to seal it.

Unroll the bamboo mat and place the roll on a cutting board, seam side down. Wet a serrated knife with water and cut the roll into 6 even pieces. Repeat for remaining rolls.

sea vegetable pâté

This pâté is even better if made a day ahead and refrigerated, giving the flavors more time to blend. Serve with salty crackers or fresh bread.

START TO FINISH:

30 minutes

Makes 1½ cups

½ cup dried hiziki seaweed

3 tablespoons toasted sesame seed oil

2–3 tablespoons soy sauce

¼ cup apple juice

2 scallions, minced

2 cloves garlic, minced

1 tablespoon grated fresh ginger

½ tablespoon lemon juice

Rinse the hiziki in a mesh strainer under cold water several minutes. Transfer to a bowl and cover with 2 cups water. Let stand 15 minutes or until soft.

Drain the hiziki in the mesh strainer and rinse under cold water several minutes.

In a medium skillet, heat 1½ tablespoons sesame oil over a medium-high flame. Add the hiziki and soy sauce and sauté 5 minutes.

Add the apple juice and enough water to cover the hiziki. Bring to a boil and cook until all liquid has evaporated. Set aside.

In a small skillet, use the remaining oil to lightly sauté the scallions and garlic 4 minutes.

Transfer the hiziki mixture, scallion mixture, ginger and lemon juice to a food processor. Pulse until nearly smooth.

The pâté can be eaten immediately, but for best flavor chill 1 hour, then let come to room temperature before serving.

susty's super tofu salad

In the middle of nowhere New Hampshire (Northwood, actually) there is a wonderful cafe called Susty's. This self-proclaimed home of "Radical Vegan Foods" works diligently to demonstrate that vegetarian food that tastes and looks great need not be difficult to make.

The folks at Susty's roll this amazing tofu salad in flatbread and ship the wonderful sandwiches to natural food stores all over New England. There is simply no beating this salad-in-a-sandwich. It also makes a great dip for carrot sticks or crackers.

START TO FINISH:
10 minutes
Makes about 3 cups,
or enough for
4 sandwiches

TIP: Use only extra-firm tofu for this recipe.

For variety, add chopped bell peppers, 1 tablespoon Dijon mustard or 1 tablepoon minced jalapeño peppers to the salad.

1   **pound extra-firm tofu**
⅓   **cup soy mayonnaise**
3   **tablespoons nutritional yeast flakes**
1   **large carrot, finely grated**
1   **small onion, minced**
3   **tablespoons minced fresh parsley**
   Sea salt and freshly ground black pepper, to taste

Finely crumble the tofu into a bowl. Add remaining ingredients and mix well.

For a smoother salad, combine all ingredients in a food processor and pulse until just combined.

roasted eggplant and mushroom pâté

Roasted vegetables give this pâté a wonderful depth of flavor.

START TO FINISH:

2 hours

(20 minutes active)

Makes about 3 cups

TIP: This is best made
the night before and
allowed to chill. We serve
it as the centerpiece
of a tray of fruit and
crackers. Also try it as
a sandwich spread.

3 tablespoons extra-virgin olive oil, plus additional
for brushing tempeh

1 large eggplant

1 small onion

8 ounces button mushrooms

1 8-ounce package tempeh (any variety)

1⅔ cups roasted cashews

⅓ cup sweet white miso

⅓ cup tahini

1-inch piece fresh ginger

½ teaspoon allspice

2 tablespoons soy sauce

1 tablespoon lemon juice

Freshly ground black pepper, to taste

Preheat the oven to 350°F. Coat the bottom of a large baking dish with oil.
Cut off the top of the eggplant, then cut it in half lengthwise. Place each
half, cut side down, in the baking dish.

Cut the onion into large chunks. Clean and stem the mushrooms. Cut the
tempeh into 6 pieces and brush lightly with oil. Add the onion, mushrooms
and tempeh to the baking dish.

Bake 45 minutes or until the eggplant is soft and the skin is starting to
brown. If the mushrooms and onion brown before the eggplant is ready,
remove from the dish and set aside while the eggplant finishes cooking.

Remove the vegetables and tempeh from the oven and cool. Scoop the flesh
of the eggplant into the bowl of a food processor. Discard the skins. Add all
remaining ingredients, including the roasted vegetables and tempeh. Pulse
until chunky smooth.

Spoon the mixture into a lightly oiled bread pan and bake at 350°F 1 hour.
Let cool completely before turning pan upside down to release pâté.

Serve chilled.

nori party mix

This nut-and-seed mixture rivals anything found in a store. And though it isn't low in fat, it is packed with calcium. This recipe assumes you are buying raw seeds and nuts. If you buy them already roasted, reduce time in the skillet to about 3 minutes.

1 cup sunflower seeds

1 cup whole almonds

1 cup shelled peanuts

1 cup cashews

6 tablespoons soy sauce

4 sheets nori seaweed, lightly toasted

½ cup raisins

Place the seeds and nuts in a mesh strainer and rinse under cool water. Transfer to a large, heavy skillet over a medium-high flame.

Stir the mixture constantly as it dries and begins to toast. Cook about 8 minutes or until the nuts and seeds begin to brown slightly.

Add the soy sauce to the pan and stir quickly to coat the mixture. This will produce a sudden burst of steam, so be careful.

Continue stirring the mixture until the soy sauce has evaporated. Transfer the mixture to a large bowl.

Crumble the nori sheets over the bowl. Mix the nori into the nuts using a wooden spoon. Mix in the raisins. Let cool 20 minutes before serving.

START TO FINISH:
30 minutes
Makes 4½ cups

TIP: Toasting brings out the flavor of nori. To toast, grip a sheet with a pair of tongs and wave it for about 30 seconds over a gas burner set at medium-high. If you have an electric range, turn the burner to high. Nori becomes shiny and brittle when toasted. Seasoned nori flakes, available at most natural food stores, can be used to eliminate the toasting step.

tamari-roasted pumpkin seeds

These salty, crunchy seeds are more addictive than popcorn. Pumpkin seeds, also called pepitas, are popular in Mexican cooking. These are delicious eaten alone or sprinkled over a bowl of squash soup or corn chowder, tossed into a salad or ground up and added to a vinaigrette.

1 cup raw hulled pumpkin seeds

2–3 tablespoons tamari or soy sauce

Place the pumpkin seeds in a mesh strainer and rinse under cold water. Gently shake the strainer to remove excess water. Set aside to drip-dry several minutes.

While the seeds drain, heat a large, heavy skillet over a medium-high flame until hot. To test whether the skillet is hot enough, wet your fingers with a few drops of water and sprinkle the drops into the skillet. If the water instantly bubbles, the skillet is ready.

Add the pumpkin seeds and use a wooden spoon to spread evenly. Stirring continuously, dry roast the seeds until they begin to puff up and brown lightly.

Add the tamari to the pan. Stir the seeds quickly to ensure even coating. The tamari will steam and evaporate quickly.

Continue stirring until the tamari has completely evaporated, then immediately transfer the seeds to a bowl. Residual heat in the pan can burn the seeds.

START TO FINISH:

10 minutes

Makes 6 servings

TIP: Be sure to purchase raw hulled pumpkin seeds (the white shell removed). Adjust the amount of tamari to taste; tamari is quite salty. This process can be used for just about any raw seeds or nuts. Almonds are particularly good.

corn crisps

These chips are a great alternative to packaged corn chips—and you get to control the seasonings. Want them spicy? Sprinkle with paprika and chili powder. Savory more your style? Try dried dill, rosemary and onion or garlic powder. The chips go great with Peach Salsa (recipe p. 154) or Spicy Creamy Hummus (recipe p. 4).

⅔   cup freeze dried corn kernels (sold as a snack food in natural food stores)

2   cups coarse cornmeal

2   teaspoons sea salt, plus additional for salting the finished chips

1   teaspoon corn oil

5   cups boiling water

Preheat the oven to 400°F.

Place the corn in a food processor and pulse briefly, about 3 seconds or until the kernels are broken but not finely ground.

Combine the kernels, cornmeal, salt and seasonings (if you wish to incorporate them in the batter) in a medium bowl. Add the oil and water and mix well.

Let stand 10 minutes or until thickened.

While dough rests, lightly oil a large baking sheet. Drop dough by the tablespoonful onto the baking sheet, leaving 1 inch between chips. If sprinkling seasoning over the chips, do so now.

Bake 30 minutes or until lightly browned. Lightly sprinkle the chips with salt. Let cool 5 minutes before transferring to a large bowl.

START TO FINISH:
40 minutes
(10 minutes active)
Makes 6 dozen chips
(about 4–6 servings)

TIP: Seasonings can be mixed into the chip batter, or sprinkled over them just before baking, depending on your preference.

Some good seasoning combinations include: 1 teaspoon each of garlic powder and paprika; 1 teaspoon each dried dill and onion powder; 2 teaspoons very finely minced fresh rosemary; or 1 teaspoon paprika and ½ teaspoon chili powder.

savory plantain chips

We first tasted a high-fat version of these banana-like chips at a wonderful Cuban restaurant. Our goal was to lose the fat without sacrificing the flavor. We made a healthier version by baking the plantain slices instead of frying them.

START TO FINISH:

20 minutes

Makes 4 servings

TIP: When selecting plantains, be sure to choose green ones. The riper yellow ones are too soft to slice cleanly. Also, be sure to brown them well during cooking or they will become soggy as they cool. Keep in mind that cooking time can vary according to the moisture content of the fruit and the thickness of the slices.

Extra-virgin olive oil

2 large green plantains

1 teaspoon sea salt

Pinch of garlic powder

½ fresh lime

Preheat the oven to 350°F. Lightly coat a baking sheet with olive oil.

Peel the plantains and slice into ¼-inch rounds. Place the slices on the baking sheet.

Mix the salt and garlic powder in a small shaker and sprinkle lightly over the plantain slices.

Bake 12 minutes or until lightly browned. Remove the slices and cool on a wire rack. To serve, sprinkle with lime juice.

breads

flatbread

As temptations go, nothing is quite as tantalizing as freshly baked bread. But baking from scratch can take at least 4 hours from start to finish. That's great for weekends, but we wanted something we could throw together after work. So we came up with this quick flatbread, which can be whipped up in just minutes. The bread comes out of the oven hot and chewy and is great for sandwich wraps. Or tear it into smaller pieces for dipping in Spicy Creamy Hummus (recipe p. 4) and Tapenade (recipe p. 2).

START TO FINISH:
15 minutes
Makes six 8-inch
flatbreads

TIP: Though we generally prefer whole wheat to white flour, we recommend white for this recipe. Whole wheat makes these breads too dense and dry. Also try cooking these on the grill.

1½   **cups unbleached white flour, plus extra for kneading**

½–¾ **cup water**

½   **teaspoon sea salt**

       Extra-virgin olive oil

Combine the flour, water and salt in a large mixing bowl. Mix together with a wooden spoon, then knead the dough with your hands in the bowl about 3 minutes or until the mixture forms a heavy, slightly sticky ball. Add more water if needed, but be careful not to overdo it; the dough should be dense and slightly tacky.

Turn the dough out onto a lightly floured surface. Knead another minute. The dough should be mostly dry to the touch. If not, sprinkle 1 tablespoon of flour on the work surface and knead the dough an additional 30 seconds.

Shape the dough into a log roughly 6 inches long. Cut the log into 6 pieces.

Flatten each piece with a rolling pin into an 8-inch round or until about ¼ inch thick. Use additional flour on the work surface if needed to prevent sticking.

Lightly coat a large skillet or griddle with oil and heat over a medium flame.

Place a dough round in the skillet and cook until it begins to puff and is golden on the bottom, 1–2 minutes. Flip and cook the bread on the other side 1 minute. Repeat with remaining rounds.

START TO FINISH:

20 minutes

Makes 4 servings,

3 pieces per serving

TIP: To make pressing the dough easier, place each dough ball between two pieces of parchment paper, then press flat.

oat flatbread

A friend in Scotland taught us this version of traditional Scottish oat farls. The rustic bread is a cross between a biscuit and a cracker. It is great on its own, with soup or slathered with pâté.

1	teaspoon sesame seeds
1	cup rolled oats
¼	cup unbleached white flour
1	tablespoon extra-virgin olive oil
¼	teaspoon sea salt
½–¾	cup boiling water
1	tablespoon chopped scallions

Toast seeds in a hot, dry skillet, stirring constantly until they begin to pop and are lightly browned.

Place the seeds, oats, flour, oil and salt in a food processor. Process until the mixture resembles a coarse meal, about 10 seconds. Add the water and scallions and process several more seconds until well blended.

Moisten hands with water and remove the dough from the processor. Form the dough into 3 balls. Press each ball into a 6-inch round about ¼ inch thick. Cut each round into quarters.

Lightly oil a cast-iron skillet and heat over a medium flame. Cook 4 quarters at a time, about 3 minutes per side. Add more oil to the skillet between batches, if needed.

nutty flatbread

Pistachios and sesame, flax and poppy seeds give this flatbread a great nutty flavor. Try one as a sandwich wrap with greens, or tear it into pieces and dip in hummus.

¼	cup sesame seeds
¼	cup finely crushed pistachio nuts
1	tablespoon flax seeds
1	teaspoon poppy seeds
1½	cups unbleached white flour, plus additional for kneading
½	teaspoon sea salt
½–¾	cup water
2	tablespoons extra-virgin olive oil, plus extra to brush the pan

Heat a large, heavy skillet over a medium flame. Add the sesame seeds and pistachio nuts and toast, stirring constantly, until just lightly browned, about 4 minutes. Transfer the seeds and nuts to a large mixing bowl and set aside to cool, about 5 minutes.

Add the flax seeds and poppy seeds to the mixing bowl. Add the flour and salt, and mix to combine. Add the water and oil and mix together with a wooden spoon, then knead the dough with your hands in the bowl until the dough is heavy and slightly sticky, about 3 minutes. Add more water if needed, but don't overdo it; the dough should be dense and slightly tacky.

Turn the dough out onto a lightly floured surface and knead about 2 minutes, using additional flour on the work surface if needed to prevent sticking.

Shape the dough into a log about 6 inches long. Cut the log with a sharp knife into 6 pieces. Flatten each piece with a rolling pin into an 8-inch round about ¼ inch thick. You may need additional flour on the work surface to prevent sticking.

Lightly brush the skillet with oil and heat over a medium flame. Cook the rounds, one at a time, until they puff and are golden on the bottom, about 1–2 minutes. Flip and cook 1 minute on the other side.

START TO FINISH:
20 minutes
Makes six 8-inch flatbreads

TIP: Any small nuts or seeds can be substituted. Try almond slivers and poppy seeds, or finely ground cashews.

cornbread

Eat this bread warm and slathered with soy margarine, or use as a base for stuffing. This recipe also makes great muffins.

START TO FINISH:

40 minutes

Makes 1 loaf

TIP: The recipe calls for 1 cup corn kernels, but we can't get enough of them. Up to 1½ cups can be added for extra texture and flavor. For a stronger taste of the Southwest, add 1–2 tablespoons diced jalapeño peppers.

The kuzu or agar powder acts as a natural binder, replacing eggs. Cornstarch can be substituted 1:1 for kuzu. If you prefer a more crumbly cornbread, the kuzu can be omitted.

1½	tablespoons kuzu or ⅜ teaspoon agar powder
1	cup whole wheat pastry flour or unbleached all-purpose white flour
1	cup cornmeal
2	teaspoons baking powder
½	teaspoon baking soda
2	tablespoons sugar
1½	teaspoons chili powder
1	teaspoon sea salt
1⅓	cups soy or rice milk
1	teaspoon lemon juice
3	tablespoons corn oil or extra-virgin olive oil
1	cup fresh or frozen corn kernels

Preheat the oven to 375°F. Lightly oil a 9 × 9-inch baking pan.

Pulverize the kuzu with the back of a spoon in a small bowl. Whisk together the kuzu and remaining dry ingredients in a large mixing bowl.

Make a well in the center and add the soy or rice milk, lemon juice and oil. Stir until combined. Add the corn and stir until mixed.

Pour the batter into the prepared pan and bake until cornbread is golden, about 30–35 minutes. Place on a wire rack and cool completely.

pumpkin bread

This moist, sweet bread is best fresh from the oven. Go for a squash theme and serve it with a steaming bowl of Hearty Autumn Squash and Bean Stew (recipe p. 59).

START TO FINISH:
1 hour, 15 minutes
Makes one 9 × 5-inch loaf

  2 tablespoons corn oil

  1 medium banana, very ripe

  6 ounces soft, silken tofu

  ⅓ cup maple syrup

  ⅓ cup vanilla rice milk

  8 ounces canned pumpkin

  1¾ cups unbleached white flour

  ⅓ cup sugar or maple syrup crystals

  1 teaspoon baking soda

  ½ teaspoon baking powder

  ½ teaspoon sea salt

  ½ teaspoon cinnamon

  ½ teaspoon ground cloves

  ⅔ cup golden raisins

  ½ teaspoon cider vinegar

TIP: Raisins, whether baked in bread or scattered over a salad, are best if plumped first by soaking them in warm water. Soak each cup of raisins in several cups of warm water for 20 minutes. Drain well before using.

Preheat the oven to 350°F. Lightly oil a standard 9 × 5-inch loaf pan.

In a food processor, combine the oil, banana, tofu, maple syrup, rice milk and pumpkin. Purée until smooth.

In a mixing bowl, sift together the flour, sugar, baking soda and powder, salt, cinnamon and cloves.

Combine the dry mixture with the liquid mixture to make a thick, smooth batter. Fold in the raisins. Quickly stir in the vinegar. Pour the batter into the prepared pan.

Bake 1 hour or until a toothpick inserted in the center of the loaf comes out clean. Cool in the pan 10 minutes. Remove the loaf and cool another 15 minutes on a wire rack before slicing.

fluffy biscuits

These versatile biscuits are great with any dish that has sauce to be mopped up. We use natural shortening to give them a traditional flavor. Unlike regular shortenings, natural versions aren't hydrogenated. They instead use tropical oils, such as palm oil, which are solid at room temperature.

START TO FINISH:

30 minutes

Makes 12 biscuits

TIP: Sweeten the biscuit batter with a few table-spoons of brown rice syrup or maple syrup for a dessert shortcake, great with fresh straw-berries.

Biscuits are best served warm but will remain fresh a day or two if covered. They also can be tightly wrapped and frozen.

2	**cups unbleached white flour**
2	**cups whole wheat pastry flour**
2	**tablespoons baking powder**
1 ½	**teaspoons sea salt**
2	**teaspoons cider vinegar**
1½	**cups soy/rice milk blend**
½	**cup natural shortening**

Preheat the oven to 450°F. Lightly oil a large baking sheet.

Combine the flours, baking powder and salt in a large mixing bowl. In a small bowl, combine the vinegar and the soy/rice milk.

Cut the shortening into the flour mixture using 2 knives until a coarse meal forms. Add the milk/vinegar mixture and gently mix together with a wooden spoon until evenly moist. Don't over-mix.

Roll out the dough on a lightly floured surface until about ½ inch thick. Cut rounds out of the dough with a biscuit cutter, pressing straight down without twisting the cutter.

Place the rounds on the prepared baking sheet. Bake 12 minutes or until lightly browned.

salads

roasted rosemary and honey potato salad

Here is a healthy twist on the all-American summer comfort food. Rather than load the dish with cholesterol and fat, this salad uses fresh rosemary, honey, vinegar and mustard to accent crispy, roasted potatoes.

START TO FINISH:

45 minutes

Makes 8 servings

TIP: For interest, use a variety of potatoes, such as purple, red and yellow.

If you don't eat honey, maple and brown rice syrups work nicely, too.

3   pounds new potatoes, cut into quarters

2   tablespoons, plus ½ cup extra-virgin olive oil

1   green bell pepper, seeded and diced

1   red bell pepper, seeded and diced

1   orange bell pepper, seeded and diced

3   medium carrots, ends trimmed, cut into matchsticks

4   celery stalks, finely chopped

¼   cup fresh chives, diced

4   tablespoons finely chopped fresh rosemary leaves

¼   cup apple cider vinegar

⅓   cup Dijon mustard

3   tablespoons honey

Preheat the oven to 425°F.

Bring about 1 inch of water to a boil in a large saucepan fitted with a steamer basket. Add the potatoes, cover and steam until just tender, about 12 minutes.

Use 2 tablespoons of oil to coat a jelly roll pan. Transfer the potatoes to the pan and toss to coat with oil. Bake 5 minutes. Switch the oven to broil and cook 2–3 minutes more or until the potatoes start to brown and crisp. Watch carefully to avoid burning. Remove pan from the oven and cool potatoes 15 minutes.

Combine the peppers, carrots and celery in a large bowl. Add the potatoes and chives and toss to combine.

For the dressing, combine the rosemary, vinegar, mustard, remaining oil and honey in a blender. Process until combined, then pour over salad and toss. Chill 1 hour. Toss again before serving.

roasted tempeh salad with lemon-vinegar sauce

This is an easy, low-fat summer salad packed with protein and crisp, brightly colored vegetables.

½ cup brown rice vinegar

3 tablespoons lemon juice

2 tablespoons maple syrup

1 8-ounce package tempeh, cut into 6 strips

1 tablespoon sunflower oil

4 cups leafy greens or leaf lettuce

8 cherry tomatoes, cut in halves

1 red bell pepper, seeded and roughly diced

1 orange bell pepper, seeded and roughly diced

1 cup loosely packed fresh basil leaves

1 carrot, shaved

½ cup extra-virgin olive oil

½ teaspoon freshly ground pepper

½ teaspoon sea salt

In a small bowl, whisk together the vinegar, lemon juice and maple syrup. Lay the tempeh strips in a deep dish and pour marinade over the top. Cover and refrigerate several hours.

Heat the sunflower oil in a skillet over a medium-high flame. Remove the tempeh strips from the marinade and place them in the pan, reserving the marinade. Let the tempeh brown, then turn the strips and repeat, about 2 minutes per side.

While the tempeh cooks, combine the vegetables in a serving bowl or arrange on individual plates. Place the tempeh strips over the salad.

For the dressing, combine the remaining marinade with the olive oil, pepper and salt in a small bowl or jar with a lid. Shake or whisk well and pour over salad.

START TO FINISH:
20 minutes active (plus several hours marinating)
Makes 4 servings

TIP: We usually begin marinating the tempeh before we leave for work in the morning. When we come home for lunch or dinner, all we need to do is throw the vegetables together while the tempeh crisps in the pan.

To shave a carrot, run a vegetable peeler along the length of the carrot, creating a thin, wide ribbon.

panzanella (tomato and bread salad)

The Italians really know salads. This hearty combination of bread, tomatoes and olive oil shames those limp iceberg wrecks so many restaurants try to pass off as salad. This also is a great way to use day-old bread.

1 pound very ripe tomatoes (Roma are excellent)

   Kosher salt or coarse sea salt

1 pound day-old bread, cut into 1-inch cubes

½ cup extra-virgin olive oil

4 tablespoons balsamic vinegar

1 red onion, diced

2 tablespoons capers

10 fresh basil leaves, cut into ribbons

2 teaspoons chopped fresh oregano leaves

1 tablespoon chopped fresh parsley

   Sea salt and freshly ground black pepper, to taste

Cut the tomatoes into small chunks and place in a mesh strainer over the sink or a large bowl. Add 1 tablespoon of salt and gently work through with your fingers. Drain the tomatoes about 10 minutes.

Place the bread cubes in a large bowl.

In another bowl, whisk together the oil and vinegar. Add the onions, capers, tomatoes and half the herbs. Toss to combine and let stand 10 minutes.

Add the tomato mixture to the bread. Add the remaining herbs and toss to combine. Season with salt and pepper.

START TO FINISH:

30 minutes

Makes 4 servings

TIP: Use a white country-style bread. Avoid anything sliced or soft. The bread also should be fairly simple—nothing with excessive seeds or any fruits.

For variation, substitute 4 tablespoons diced Kalamata olives for the capers.

Don't make this salad more than 30 minutes ahead of time, as the bread will become too soggy. You can prepare the bread cubes and tomato mixture early, but wait to combine them until just before serving.

sesame carrot salad

Some of the best flavors to accent raw vegetables include ginger, vinegar and hearty tahini, a paste made from ground sesame seeds. This recipe has them all.

START TO FINISH:

20 minutes

Makes 6 servings

TIP: During winter, make just the dressing and drizzle it over steamed vegetables, such as broccoli, cauliflower or green beans.

This salad also is good with freshly made croutons. To make croutons, lightly brush slices of whole wheat bread or a hearty peasant-style bread with olive oil and bake at 350°F 10–15 minutes or until dry and crunchy. Crumble or cut the bread into cubes and toss with salad.

¾ pound mixed salad greens, or kale and chard leaves, finely chopped

2 medium tomatoes, diced

3 medium carrots, ends trimmed, cut into matchsticks

1 medium cucumber, sliced

1 red bell pepper, seeded and diced

2 tablespoons sesame seeds

3 tablespoons mirin

2 tablespoons brown rice vinegar

1 tablespoon soy sauce

1 tablespoon Dijon mustard

1 teaspoon grated fresh ginger

2 tablespoons tahini

In a large bowl, toss together the greens, tomatoes, carrots, the cucumber and pepper.

Combine the remaining ingredients, except the sesame seeds, in a food processor or blender and purée until smooth.

Drizzle the dressing over the salad. Top with a sprinkle of sesame seeds.

pasta and sweet vegetable salad

When it's hot outside and you want to get out of the kitchen fast, this delicious and healthy salad has you eating in 15 minutes.

¾ pound ziti pasta or other small pasta variety

¼ cup finely chopped fresh basil, plus ½ cup

¼ cup balsamic vinegar

2 tablespoons extra-virgin olive oil

1 tablespoon Dijon mustard

2 medium tomatoes, diced

½ cup corn kernels

½ cup chopped red onion

Sea salt and freshly ground black pepper, to taste

Bring a large saucepan of lightly salted water to a boil. Add pasta and cook until tender, about 8 minutes. Rinse with cool water, drain and set aside.

In a small bowl, whisk together ¼ cup basil with the vinegar, oil and mustard. Set aside.

In a large bowl, combine the remaining ingredients, including the pasta and remaining ½ cup of chopped basil. Add dressing and toss. Season with salt and pepper.

START TO FINISH:
15 minutes
Makes 6 servings

TIP: To spice this up, substitute wasabi for the mustard, but go easy. Try ½ teaspoon of wasabi paste first. It doesn't take much wasabi to give plenty of kick.

START TO FINISH:

45 minutes

Makes 4 servings

TIP: The stalks in kale and other hardy cool-weather greens are edible but tough. Use a sharp paring knife to remove them before chopping the leaves.

warm greens salad

This is a salad of wonderful contrasts—warm sautéed greens and onions tossed with cool tomatoes and cucumbers, crunchy fresh croutons paired with gently seared tofu and, of course, a tangy sweet-and-sour dressing.

SALAD:

- 4 large slices hearty white bread
- 3 tablespoons extra-virgin olive oil
- ½ cup cider vinegar
- ⅓ cup brown rice syrup or maple syrup
- 1 teaspoon curry powder
- 2 medium onions, diced
- ½ pound baked, seasoned tofu, cut into ½-inch cubes
- ¼ cup toasted sesame seed oil
- 1 pound kale, stalks removed, cut into thin ribbons
- 3 cups loosely packed mesclun mix or other salad greens
- 3 medium tomatoes, coarsely diced
- 1 medium cucumber, sliced into half rounds
- ¼ cup pistachio pieces

DRESSING:

- ¼ cup cider vinegar
- ¼ cup maple syrup
- 2 teaspoons Dijon mustard
- 1 tablespoon ketchup

Preheat the oven to 350°F. Cut the bread into 1-inch squares. Use 1 tablespoon of the olive oil to lightly coat a baking sheet.

Arrange the bread cubes on the sheet. Drizzle the remaining oil over the cubes. Bake 10 minutes or until the croutons are crisp and slightly browned.

Meanwhile, whisk together the vinegar, brown rice syrup and curry powder in a small bowl. Place the onions in a medium bowl. Add the vinegar mixture and toss to coat. Cover and refrigerate 20 minutes.

Heat the sesame oil in a large saucepan over a medium-high flame. Add the tofu and cook until slightly crisp, turning to brown all sides. Remove the tofu to paper towels to drain.

Transfer the onions and half of the marinade to a large skillet. Simmer until the liquid is reduced to a thick syrup and the onions are translucent, about 10 minutes.

Add the kale to the skillet and sauté until limp, 1–2 minutes.

In a large serving bowl, toss together the mesclun greens with the kale, onions and 2–3 tablespoons of any liquid remaining in the skillet. Add the tofu, tomatoes and cucumbers and toss again.

Top the salad with pistachio pieces and croutons.

For the dressing, whisk together all ingredients. Drizzle sparingly over the salad.

italian salad with apples and raisins

The sweetness of the raisins and the crunch of the pine nuts in this classic Tuscan salad make dressing almost unnecessary. A simple drizzle of oil and vinegar is all that is needed.

START TO FINISH:

30 minutes

Makes 6 servings

TIP: Pine nuts, like most seeds and nuts, taste best after a quick toasting. Place the pine nuts in a heavy skillet and sauté, stirring often, over a medium-high flame until just golden, about 5 minutes. They also can be baked 10 minutes in a 350°F oven.

Instead of raisins, try dried or fresh figs cut into quarters.

1 cup raisins

¾ pound mixed greens or baby spinach leaves

2 apples, cored and sliced into half-moons

2 medium carrots, ends trimmed, cut into matchsticks

3 tablespoons pine nuts, lightly toasted

1 tablespoon sea salt

3 tablespoons balsamic vinegar

Extra-virgin olive oil, to taste

Soak the raisins in warm water 20 minutes or until soft and plump. Drain and gently squeeze to remove excess water.

Toss the greens, apples and carrots together in a large bowl. Sprinkle the pine nuts, raisins and salt over the salad.

Drizzle the vinegar over the salad, followed by the oil.

seitan and soba noodle salad

This warm salad is an add-whatever-you-have sort of dish. We call for carrots, broccoli, cauliflower and green beans, but let your produce section and imagination be your guide.

START TO FINISH:

30 minutes

Makes 2–4 servings

TIP: Also try this dish chilled. Throw it together in advance, then either let it come to room temperature or chill it in the refrigerator.

1   medium carrot, ends trimmed, cut into thin rounds

2   cups broccoli florets

1   cup cauliflower florets

1   cup green beans, cut to 1-inch lengths

8   ounces soba noodles

4   tablespoons toasted sesame seed oil

4   tablespoons soy sauce

4   tablespoons vegetable broth or water

1   tablespoon tahini

1   teaspoon lime juice

1   tablespoon mirin

½   teaspoon sea salt

½   pound seitan, cubed

    Sesame seeds, for garnish

Bring a large saucepan of water to a boil. Using a slotted spoon, place the carrot rounds in the water and blanch 1 minute. Remove carrots and set aside in a bowl.

Repeat blanching with broccoli, cauliflower and green beans, one vegetable at a time, 1 minute cooking for each. Cover vegetables and set aside.

Bring a medium saucepan of lightly salted water to a boil. Cook the soba noodles until tender, about 6 minutes. Drain and set aside.

In a large skillet, heat the sesame oil over a medium flame. Whisk in the soy sauce, broth, tahini, lime juice, mirin and salt. Reduce heat and simmer 1 minute.

Add the noodles and stir to coat with sauce. Add the seitan and cook 3 minutes or until warm.

To serve, arrange the vegetables on individual plates and top with noodles and seitan. Sprinkle with sesame seeds.

spicy asian noodle salad

A fast and easy tossed noodle salad that packs plenty of taste. It's great warm or cold. Pair it with fresh spring rolls and a bit of sushi for a great Asian dinner.

8	ounces soba or udon noodles
½	cup chopped fresh cilantro
6	scallions, chopped
2	tablespoons soy sauce
2	tablespoons sesame oil
1	tablespoon lime juice
1	small fresh jalapeño chili or other hot pepper, seeds removed
¼	teaspoon paprika
1	teaspoon mirin
¼	cup dry-roasted peanuts

Bring a medium saucepan of lightly salted water to a boil. Cook noodles until tender, about 6 minutes. Drain, rinse with cool water and set aside to drip-dry.

Meanwhile, combine the cilantro, half the scallions, soy sauce, oil, lime juice, chili, paprika and mirin in a blender or food processor. Purée until smooth.

Transfer the noodles to a large serving bowl. Add the dressing and toss to coat. Garnish with peanuts and remaining scallions.

START TO FINISH:
30 minutes
Makes 4 servings

TIP: Raw peanuts are easy to roast. Preheat the oven to 350°F. Spread the nuts on a cookie sheet and bake 10 minutes or until they just begin to brown.

When seeding jalapeño peppers, it is best to wear disposable rubber gloves. The oil in the peppers burns. And be careful not to touch any-one, including yourself.

START TO FINISH:

**1 hour, 15 minutes
(15 minutes active)
Makes 4 servings**

TIP: Add interest to
noodle dishes by using
unusual pasta shapes
and colors.

zippy zingy pasta shell salad

*Here's proof that just a few simple ingredients are easily transformed into a
wonderful meal.*

*Use whatever vegetables you have, including leftovers. Broccoli and cauliflower
are especially good. Chill this dish prior to serving so the flavors develop.*

4 cups small pasta shells

1 cup frozen corn kernels

1 cup frozen peas

2 celery stalks, diced

1 carrot, ends trimmed, cut in half lengthwise, then diced

4 tablespoons chopped fresh dill

½ cup cider vinegar

¼ cup extra-virgin olive oil

2 tablespoons nutritional yeast flakes

Bring a large saucepan of lightly salted water to a boil and cook pasta until
tender, about 8 minutes. Drain and set aside.

While the pasta cooks, place the frozen corn and peas in a large mixing
bowl. Transfer the hot pasta from the strainer into the mixing bowl and toss
with the corn and peas. Add the celery, carrots and dill and mix to combine.

Combine the vinegar, oil and yeast flakes in a blender and purée until
smooth. Pour the dressing over the salad and toss to coat.

Cover the salad with plastic wrap and chill 1 hour. Toss again before serving.

chickpea and red pepper salad

This salad easily stands on its own, or it can be spooned into pita pockets for a Mediterranean sandwich.

START TO FINISH:
15 minutes
Makes 6 servings

Two 15-ounce cans chickpeas, drained and rinsed

1 medium cucumber, seeded and chopped

1 red bell pepper, seeded and diced

1 cup corn kernels

1 tablespoon extra-virgin olive oil

1 tablespoon balsamic vinegar

2 tablespoons soy sauce

½ teaspoon mustard powder

½ teaspoon red chili paste

1 clove garlic, minced

6 cups baby salad greens

Combine chickpeas, cucumber, pepper and corn in a large bowl. In a small bowl, whisk together the remaining ingredients, except the salad greens.

Toss the dressing with the chickpea mixture to coat. Arrange 1 cup of greens on each serving plate and top with the chickpeas.

TIP: To seed a cucumber, cut it in half lengthwise. Cut the length of the cucumber into manageable 4 or 5-inch pieces. One at a time, hold each piece in the palm of your hand, cut side up. Use a spoon to scrape out the seeds.

spicy orange salad

Try this refreshing salad during summer, or drizzle the dressing over steamed vegetables and rice during cooler months.

START TO FINISH:

20 minutes

Makes 6 servings

TIP: The theme of this salad is easy to change. For a fall feel, substitute apple chunks for the oranges and apple juice or cider for the juice in the dressing.

¾ pound mixed salad greens

1 small cucumber, sliced into rounds

1 cup fresh green beans, cut into 1-inch sections

½ cup dry-roasted cashews

2 oranges, peeled, separated into sections, each section halved crosswise

¼ cup apple cider vinegar

⅓ cup orange juice

1 tablespoon chopped fresh dill

1 teaspoon honey or brown rice syrup

½ teaspoon paprika

½ teaspoon soy sauce

½ teaspoon sea salt

⅓ cup extra-virgin olive oil

In a large bowl toss the greens, cucumber and green beans. Top with cashews and orange sections.

For the dressing, place all remaining ingredients in a glass jar with a lid and shake. Drizzle dressing over salad and serve.

gingery asian pressed salad

This unusual and flavorful Asian salad will remind some people of coleslaw, others of kimchee.

The technique used here is a type of quick pickling, which makes cabbage and cucumbers easier to digest.

SALAD:

¼	cup golden raisins
½	head small cabbage, thinly shredded
1	cucumber, peeled and thinly sliced
4–5	radishes, thinly sliced
1	medium carrot, ends trimmed
¼	cup umeboshi vinegar
1	large apple
¼	cup dry-roasted sunflower seeds

DRESSING:

¼	cup tahini
	1-inch piece fresh ginger
¼	cup mirin
1	teaspoon soy sauce
2	tablespoons orange juice
1	tablespoon apricot all-fruit jam

START TO FINISH:

1 hour, 20 minutes (20 minutes active)

Makes 4 servings

TIP: It is important to use a large mixing bowl to make this salad. You will need to place a plate on top of the salad to press it.

Place the raisins in a small bowl and cover with warm water. Let stand 20 minutes or until soft and plump. Drain and set aside.

Combine the cabbage, cucumber and radish slices in a large mixing bowl. Use a vegetable peeler to shave the carrot into the bowl.

Add the vinegar to the vegetables. Use your hands to massage the vinegar into the vegetables, squeezing gently, about 3 minutes.

Place a plate that fits into the bowl on top of the vegetables. Weigh down the plate with something heavy, such as a pitcher filled with water. Let stand 1 hour.

While the salad presses, make the dressing. Combine all ingredients in a blender or food processor and purée until smooth. Cover and refrigerate until ready to use.

Once the salad has pressed, remove the weight, but leave the plate in place. Holding the plate down with one hand, tip the bowl over the sink to drain any liquid.

Transfer the pickled vegetables to a medium bowl, squeezing gently with your hands to remove any remaining liquid.

Slice the apple in half and core. Cut each piece into thin half-moon slices. Add the slices to the salad.

To serve, toss the salad with several tablespoons of the dressing or to taste. Garnish with raisins and sunflower seeds.

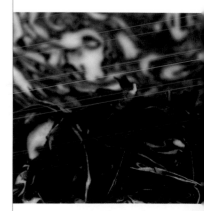

tangy avocado and rice salad

It's tough to beat avocados for their creamy texture. In this salad, they are complemented by a tangy orange vinaigrette and crunchy cashews.

START TO FINISH:

20 minutes

Makes 2 servings

TIP: If your cashews aren't already toasted, spread them on a baking sheet and bake in a 350°F oven 10 minutes or until they just begin to brown.

Fresh cooked rice is best for this recipe, as refrigerated rice tends to dry out and stick together too much for use in salads.

¼ cup golden raisins

2 heaping cups mixed salad greens

1 cup cooked long-grain brown rice, room temperature

2 oranges, peeled and divided into sections

1 small cucumber, peeled and thinly sliced

1 medium carrot, sliced into thin rounds

1 avocado, peeled and sliced into half moons

½ cup cashews, roasted

DRESSING

2 tablespoons apple cider vinegar

¼ cup orange juice

¼ cup extra-virgin olive oil

¼ teaspoon freshly ground black pepper

½ teaspoon sea salt

Place the raisins in a small bowl and cover with warm water. Let stand 20 minutes or until soft and plump. Drain and set aside.

While the raisins soak, toss together the rice and greens in a medium serving bowl. Add the orange, cucumber and carrot slices and toss to combine.

Arrange the avocado on top of the salad. Sprinkle with cashews and raisins.

For the dressing, combine all the ingredients in a glass jar with a lid and shake vigorously. Alternatively, whisk together in a small bowl or combine in a blender. Drizzle the dressing over the salad just before serving.

soups and stews

chilled carrot-dill soup

For a summer starter with spark, try this cold soup of carrots, fresh dill, sweet potato and a touch of ginger. The sweet potato gives the soup a thick, hearty consistency and prevents the watery taste so common in cold soups.

Never boil this soup. Allow it to simmer until the vegetables are just tender. For even more zip, add a tablespoon or two of sweet white miso when puréeing.

START TO FINISH:

30 minutes

(plus 2 hours to chill)

Makes 6 servings

TIP: Ginger can dry out and spoil if left in the refrigerator. The best way to store it is in the freezer. This also makes it easier to grate as needed.

1 **tablespoon corn oil**

1 **pound carrots, ends trimmed, cut into ¼-inch rounds**

1 **large sweet potato, peeled and finely diced or grated**

1 **medium onion, diced**

6 **cups vegetable broth**

4 **tablespoons minced fresh dill**

1-inch piece fresh ginger

Sea salt and freshly ground black pepper, to taste

Heat the oil in a large saucepan over a medium flame. Add the carrots, sweet potato and onion. Sauté about 3 minutes.

Add the broth, dill, ginger, salt and pepper and bring to a simmer. Cook 15–20 minutes or until vegetables are tender.

Transfer soup to a food processor or blender, in batches if necessary, and purée lightly. Soup should have a slightly mealy texture; do not whip the soup smooth.

Return the soup to the pot and chill 2 hours before serving.

creamy corn chowder

There is something immensely satisfying about a steaming bowl of creamy corn chowder. Its rich, thick broth loaded with crisp kernels is a wonderful way to warm up on a cool autumn afternoon.

Though this soup is best cooked slowly and gently, once it is done it stores well and can be frozen for a quick bowl of chowder whenever you need it.

START TO FINISH:

50 minutes

Makes 4–6 servings

TIP: For an especially rich take on this dish, save the corn cobs after cutting off the kernels. Place the cobs in a medium saucepan with enough water to cover. Bring to a boil, then cover, reduce heat and simmer 1 hour. Use this liquid for half of the rice milk called for in the recipe.

4	tablespoons extra-virgin olive oil
1	clove garlic, minced
1	medium onion, diced
2	medium carrots, ends trimmed, cut into thin rounds
2	medium potatoes, cut into small cubes
2	scallions, chopped
8	ears of corn or 1 pound frozen corn kernels
1	teaspoon sea salt
1½	quarts vanilla rice milk
3	tablespoons sweet white miso
	Pinch chili powder
1	teaspoon ground cumin
½	teaspoon freshly ground pepper

In a large stockpot, combine the oil, garlic, onion, carrots, potatoes and scallions and sauté over a medium flame until the onion is soft, about 6 minutes. Stir frequently to prevent the mixture from sticking, adding a few tablespoons of water as needed.

Meanwhile, use a paring knife to cut the corn kernels from the cobs by standing each ear of corn on its wide end. Place the knife against the kernels and cut downward in a sawing motion.

Add the corn and salt to the pot and cook about 3 minutes. Add enough rice milk to just cover the ingredients. Cover, reduce heat to low and simmer 20 minutes.

Place about half of the chowder in a blender and purée 30 seconds. Add the miso, chili powder, cumin and pepper and purée until the mixture is smooth. Return the soup to the pot and simmer another 5 minutes.

miso soup

In Japan, miso soup is eaten as breakfast and as a warming starter for the evening meal. It is quick and easy to make and has a savory, salty flavor.

Don't feel bound by these ingredients. Miso soup is a great repository for leftover vegetables. Use whatever you have, simmer in water until tender, then stir in the miso.

START TO FINISH:

15 minutes

Makes 2 servings

TIP: Miso is a salty paste made from fermented soy beans. It is available in a range of flavors, from beefy three-year barley to mellow white. First-timers should start with lighter colored miso, which is sweeter.

For the Japanese equivalent of chicken soup, add udon or soba noodles, or cooked rice, to make this recipe a complete meal.

In winter add 1 teaspoon of fresh grated ginger for a bit of warmth.

4	cups water
	3-inch piece dried wakame seaweed, broken into small bits
1	dried shiitake mushroom, stem removed
½	small onion, thinly sliced
¼	cup thinly sliced carrot rounds
2	ounces extra-firm, or baked, seasoned tofu, cubed
2–4	tablespoons miso (start with 2 and taste)
¼	cup sliced scallion, for garnish

Bring wakame and water to a boil in a medium saucepan. Crumble the mushroom into the water. Lower heat to a simmer.

Add the remaining ingredients, except miso and scallions. Simmer until the vegetables are tender, about 6 minutes.

Ladle about ¼ cup of the broth into a cup. Add the miso to the cup and mix until smooth. Stir the miso mixture into the soup.

Add the scallions and simmer another minute before serving.

hearty autumn squash and bean stew

This easy, stick-to-your-ribs stew can be thrown together in a slow cooker in the morning and left to simmer all day. In a pinch, the stovetop works fine in 30 minutes.

Any hard squash will do. We like buttercup, but butternut also is great. And around Halloween try pumpkin. As long as the squash you use is organic and not coated with wax, don't peel it. The skin not only is edible but also packed with vitamins.

1	medium onion, finely diced
1	cup peas
1	cup corn kernels
1	small chili, diced
1	carrot, ends trimmed, cut into thick rounds
4	medium tomatoes, diced
1	15-ounce can navy beans, with liquid
½	of a medium winter squash, seeded and cut into 1-inch chunks (about 4 cups)
1	cup cooked short-grain brown rice
1	6-ounce can tomato paste
2	teaspoons dried oregano leaves
1	teaspoon paprika
1	teaspoon ground cumin
1	teaspoon garam masala
1	teaspoon dried sage
1½	quarts vegetable broth
	Sea salt and freshly ground black pepper, to taste

In a large stockpot, combine all ingredients except the salt and pepper. The broth should just cover the other ingredients.

Bring to a boil, then cover and reduce heat to simmer. Cook 45 minutes or until the squash is easily pierced with a fork and the stew has thickened.

Before serving, season with salt and pepper to taste.

START TO FINISH:

50 minutes

Makes 6 servings

TIP: Wear rubber gloves whenever working with chili peppers, and be careful not to touch your face. The oil that gives the peppers their bite also burns skin.

autumn apple and butternut soup

Make this great soup when the leaves begin to change color and the air takes on the crispy chill of fall. It's a combination of two of the season's best offerings—apples and butternut squash.

The soup is hearty and creamy, though very low in fat. We also like to improvise some during the final simmering by tossing in just about any leftovers we can find. A favorite is roasted potatoes.

We rarely peel squash and apples when cooking them, but this recipe is an exception. In this soup, the peels can dull its otherwise brilliant color.

START TO FINISH:

45 minutes

Makes 6–8 servings

TIP: Substitute pumpkin for the squash. In the fall most grocers stock small, sweet baking pumpkins.

Watch the soup carefully during simmering, as rice milk boils over easily.

For a variation, stir in ½ cup of sweet white wine, such as a Riesling, about 3 minutes before serving.

2 ½	pounds butternut squash, peeled, seeded and cut into 1-inch chunks (roughly 8 cups)
1	medium onion, diced
2	medium apples, peeled and cut into large chunks
4	carrots, ends trimmed, cut into large chunks
5 ½	cups vanilla rice milk
2	cups corn kernels
2	tablespoons soy sauce
¼	teaspoon freshly ground pepper
1	teaspoon ground cumin
½	teaspoon cinnamon
	Pinch nutmeg
	Pinch ground cloves
2	tablespoons brown rice syrup or maple syrup
4	tablespoons sweet white miso

Bring the squash, onion, apples, carrots and rice milk to a boil in a large stockpot over a medium-high flame.

Mix in the corn, soy sauce, pepper, cumin, cinnamon, nutmeg, cloves and brown rice syrup. Return to a boil. Reduce heat to simmer, cover and cook about 20 minutes or until vegetables are soft when tested with a fork.

Transfer the vegetables to a blender or food processor, along with about a third to a half of the liquid. Reserve the remaining liquid. Purée until thick and smooth. Add the miso and purée to combine, about 20 seconds.

Return the mixture to the stockpot and mix with the remaining liquid. Simmer 5 minutes to allow flavors to combine.

pasta e fagioli zupa (pasta and beans soup)

A hearty, rich Italian soup that can be pulled together in just 30 minutes, but it only gets better the longer it simmers.

4 cups vegetable broth

2 cups water

1 15-ounce can fava beans (any bean or bean combination can be substituted), with liquid

2 celery stalks, chopped

3 medium tomatoes, diced or 14-ounce can diced tomatoes

1 teaspoon freshly ground black pepper

¼ teaspoon sea salt

2 teaspoons fresh oregano or ¾ teaspoon dried oregano

2 tablespoons extra-virgin olive oil

2 tablespoons red wine vinegar

1 teaspoon paprika

½ teaspoon red pepper flakes

8 ounces dry pasta shells

Combine all the ingredients except the pasta in a large stockpot and bring to a simmer over a medium flame. Reduce heat to low, cover and simmer 15 minutes.

Add the pasta, cover and cook until pasta is tender, about 10 minutes.

chunky mushroom chowder

This chowder is a mushroom lover's dream. It's as rich as any New England clam chowder but loaded with a variety of tasty fungi.

For a faster version, use 2 cups of cooked brown rice, and reduce the rice milk to 3 cups. Bring everything to a simmer and cook 20 minutes.

This also is a great dish to make in a slow cooker. Use the amounts listed below and cook on low 4–6 hours.

START TO FINISH:

1 hour

Makes 4 servings

TIP: Though we love fresh mushrooms, we find dried work better in soups. The drying process toughens the mushrooms just a bit— the perfect consistency for chowder.

1	cup short-grain brown rice
4	cups vanilla rice milk
¼	ounce dry maitake mushrooms
½	ounce dry lobster mushrooms
½	ounce shiitake mushrooms, stems removed
2	cups corn kernels
1	medium potato, diced
1	medium carrot, ends trimmed, sliced into thin rounds
1	teaspoon sea salt
½	teaspoon freshly ground black pepper
½	teaspoon red pepper flakes
1	tablespoon nutritional yeast flakes

Combine all the ingredients in a large stockpot. Simmer over a medium-high flame, then reduce heat to low. Cover and cook 45 minutes, stirring occasionally. After 45 minutes, test rice for tenderness.

Ladle a third of the chowder into a blender and purée until smooth. Return the chowder to the pot and stir to combine. Simmer 5 minutes.

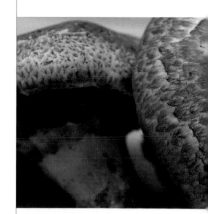

indian vegetable stew

Indian spices can bring new life to vegetable stews, adding a warmth and savory undertone lacking in most meatless soups and stews.

TIP: The flavor of just about any soup that calls for water can be given more depth by substituting vegetable broth. Be sure to reduce any salt or soy sauce called for in the recipe, as most prepared broths are high in sodium.

1½	**cups broccoli florets**
1	**cup thinly sliced carrot rounds**
2	**potatoes, cubed**
2	**bay leaves**
½	**cup flaked coconut**
6	**green chili peppers or 2 tablespoons hot pepper sauce**
1	**small onion, diced**
	½-inch piece fresh ginger
½	**teaspoon turmeric**
½	**bunch cilantro**
¼	**cup water**
½	**cup peas**
1	**large tomato, chopped**
	Sea salt, to taste
1½	**tablespoons garam masala**

Place the broccoli, carrots, potatoes and bay leaves in a heavy saucepan. Cover with water and bring to a boil. Cook until the potatoes are just tender, 6 minutes.

While the vegetables cook, combine the coconut, chili peppers, onion, ginger, turmeric and cilantro in a blender or food processor. Add ¼ cup water and purée until a fine paste forms. Set aside.

Discard the bay leaves from the vegetable mixture. Add the peas, tomato and salt to the pan. Cook another 2 minutes. Add the spice paste and stir to combine. Add the garam masala and simmer 5 minutes.

tomato and bread soup

This is a Tuscan classic that took a trip through the United States, where it picked up a bit of corn, and then stopped in Thailand, where it grabbed the amazing taste of galangal.

Galangal, one of Southeast Asia's most popular spices, has a savory and warm flavor that fits perfectly with so many Italian dishes. This new twist on the Italian favorite is rich with flavor, and just a touch of fire.

3 tablespoons extra-virgin olive oil

2 medium carrots, ends trimmed, cut into matchsticks

1 medium onion, diced

2 cups corn kernels

5 large tomatoes, diced, with juice

¼ cup chopped fresh basil leaves

1 tablespoon powdered galangal

Sea salt and freshly ground black pepper, to taste

5 cups vegetable broth

1 teaspoon paprika

½ pound loaf stale bread, cut into cubes

Combine the oil and carrots in a large stockpot and sauté over a medium flame 3–4 minutes. Add the onion and corn and sauté until onion is soft, about 6 minutes.

Stir in the tomatoes and their juice. Add the basil and galangal and bring to simmer. Season with salt and pepper.

Add the broth and paprika and increase the temperature to medium-high. Simmer 10 minutes.

Stir in the bread and cook another 2 minutes. Cover and remove soup from the stove. Let stand 15 minutes before serving to allow flavors to combine.

START TO FINISH:

45 minutes

Makes 4 servings

TIP: Powdered, fresh and dried galangal are readily available online and in spice specialty shops. In a pinch, substitute powdered ginger. The taste won't be as savory, but it will give the soup the zing it needs.

The best bread for this recipe is a hearty round peasant loaf or other heavy-crusted bread. Stale French bread also works. Avoid using sliced bread, especially white, which will disintegrate in the soup.

thai sweet potato and leek chowder

This twist on a classic dish uses Thai seasonings to give sweet potato chowder a kick. Diners with more sensitive palates should cut back on the curry paste.

½ large stalk lemon grass, cut into 2-inch lengths

2 pounds sweet potatoes, cut into ½-inch chunks

1 medium onion, diced

1 teaspoon Thai red curry paste

1 teaspoon grated fresh ginger

4 cups vegetable broth

1 14-ounce can coconut milk

1 medium leek (greens and white), finely diced

5 ounces baked, seasoned tofu, cut into ½-inch chunks

1 teaspoon sea salt

½ teaspoon freshly ground black pepper

3 scallions (green and white), diced

½ cup crushed peanuts

Gently smack the lemon grass with a mallet, a rolling pin or the side of a large chef's knife to break up the fibers and release the flavor. Combine the sweet potatoes, lemon grass, onion, curry paste, ginger, broth and coconut milk in a large stockpot.

Bring to a boil over a medium-high flame. Cover, reduce to a simmer and cook until sweet potatoes are tender, 13–15 minutes. Add the leeks during final 5 minutes of simmering.

Remove the pot from the heat and discard the lemon grass.

Transfer half the chowder to a blender or food processor, in batches if necessary, and purée until smooth. Return the chowder to the pot and stir.

Add the tofu, salt and pepper, and return the pot to the stove over a medium flame. Bring to a simmer and cook another 5 minutes to let flavors combine.

To serve, garnish with scallions and peanuts.

START TO FINISH:

45 minutes

Makes 4–6 servings

TIP: Baked tofu comes in many flavors, or you can make your own. Start with extra-firm tofu cut into ½-inch slabs. Press the slabs between kitchen towels to drain excess moisture. Marinate them 1 hour or overnight in the flavoring of your choice, then arrange on a lightly oiled baking sheet. Bake at 250°F 1–1½ hours or until tofu is dense and chewy. Use a spatula to flip the tofu every 30 minutes.

white bean soup

Try this hearty Tuscan soup for a light lunch or pair it with crusty bread and steamed greens for dinner.

1   16-ounce can white beans, such as cannellini, drained and rinsed

2   tablespoons extra-virgin olive oil

2   cloves garlic, minced

2   teaspoons fresh thyme (½ teaspoon dry)

    Sea salt and freshly ground black pepper, to taste

2   cups water

1   medium onion, roughly chopped

1   large carrot, ends trimmed, cut into thin rounds

1   stalk celery, diced

3   medium tomatoes, finely chopped, seeds and juices retained

Combine the beans and oil in a large stockpot over a medium flame. Sauté the beans 3 minutes. Add the garlic, thyme, salt and pepper and sauté another 4 minutes or until the garlic just begins to brown.

Transfer ¾ of the beans to a food processor and purée until smooth and creamy. Return mixture to the pot.

Add the water and all remaining ingredients and bring to a simmer. Cover and cook 15–20 minutes or until the carrots are tender.

START TO FINISH:

35 minutes

Makes 2–4 servings

TIP: Canned beans are a great time-saving alternative to fresh, especially in soups where the distinct and stronger flavor of fresh beans is unnecessary. Some canned beans have added salt; use a mesh strainer to drain and rinse them if you are watching your sodium.

creamy tomato and rice soup

When we lived in Germany, we fell in love with a thick, creamy tomato soup sold by a local grocer. It was rich and soothing while also bold and spicy.

After returning to the United States, we searched for years for a comparable soup. Our efforts were further complicated because we wanted a healthier version than the cream-laden one we had enjoyed overseas.

More than a decade of searching later, inspiration hit. Toasted cashews give this soup a gentle creaminess.

START TO FINISH:
30 minutes
Makes 4 servings

TIP: When shopping for cashews or other pricey nuts for use in recipes, buy the less expensive pieces rather than fancy whole nuts.

½ cup cashew pieces

6 large, ripe tomatoes

½ cup fresh basil leaves

2 tablespoons tomato paste

2 cups cooked short-grain brown rice

2 teaspoons soy sauce

2 teaspoons balsamic vinegar

1 cup vanilla rice milk

1 tablespoon minced fresh dill (*or* 1 teaspoon dry)

Sea salt and freshly ground black pepper, to taste

Preheat the oven to 350°F. Spread the cashew pieces on a baking sheet and bake 10 minutes or until just golden.

Meanwhile, cut the tomatoes into small chunks, reserving as much of the juice as possible. Place the tomato chunks and juice in a medium saucepan.

Roughly chop half the basil and add it to the pan. Bring the mixture to a simmer over a medium flame.

Add the cashews, tomato paste, 1½ cups brown rice, soy sauce, vinegar, rice milk and dill. Cover and simmer 15 minutes.

Transfer the soup to a blender, in batches if necessary, and purée until smooth. Return soup to the pan and add remaining rice and basil.

Simmer another 3 minutes over a medium flame. Season with salt and pepper. Garnish with fresh parsley or additional basil if desired.

spicy chickpea stew

Chickpeas aren't just for hummus. Serve this delicious and simple stew with couscous for a North African treat.

START TO FINISH:

1 hour

Makes 4–6 servings

TIP: Cauliflower can be a mess to cut into chunks. To keep it clean, place the entire head in a strainer and rinse under cold water. Keeping the strainer in the sink, cut the cauliflower there. Rinse the chunks again to wash away the messy bits.

3	tablespoons extra-virgin olive oil
1	medium green bell pepper, seeded and diced
½	head cauliflower, cut into small chunks
1	medium zucchini, cut into small chunks
2	medium carrots, ends trimmed, cut into thin rounds
1	cup corn kernels
1	tablespoon cumin seeds
1	teaspoon ground coriander
1	teaspoon black mustard seeds
1	small jalapeño pepper, seeded and diced
1	tablespoon grated fresh ginger
1	28-ounce can puréed tomatoes (roughly 3 cups)
1	cup tomato juice or vegetable juice
1	teaspoon honey or brown rice syrup
1	teaspoon turmeric powder
2	tablespoons chopped fresh cilantro
1	tablespoon chopped fresh oregano
1½	teaspoons garam masala
1	teaspoon sea salt
1	15-ounce can chickpeas

Preheat the oven to 200°F.

Combine 1 tablespoon oil with the bell pepper and cauliflower in a large skillet. Sauté over a medium flame 6–7 minutes, stirring frequently, until the peppers are just tender. Transfer to a baking dish and place inside the oven to keep warm.

Combine 1 tablespoon oil, zucchini, carrots and corn in the same skillet. Cook 4–5 minutes or until zucchini softens slightly. Add to the pepper and cauliflower mixture in the baking dish.

Combine the remaining oil, cumin, coriander and mustard seeds in the same skillet. Cook 1 minute over a medium flame. Add the jalapeño pepper and ginger and cook another minute. Add the tomatoes, tomato juice, honey and turmeric and bring to a simmer over a medium flame. Reduce the heat to low and add the cilantro, oregano, garam masala and salt. Simmer 20 minutes, stirring frequently. During last 5 minutes of cooking, add the chickpeas.

Pour the tomato-chickpea sauce over the pepper and cauliflower mixture. Return to the oven 5 minutes so flavors combine.

millet and sweet vegetable soup

This wonderful soup combines a host of delicate flavors—white miso, butternut squash, carrots and millet—to make a surprisingly rich soup.

	2-inch strip dried kombu seaweed
¼	cup celery, diced
1	medium yellow onion, diced
½	cup diced cabbage
1	small carrot, ends trimmed, cut into thin rounds
½	cup frozen corn kernels
¾	cup cubed butternut squash
1	cup millet, rinsed in mesh colander
2 ½	cups water
2 ½	cups vegetable broth
2	tablespoons sweet white miso
½	teaspoon sea salt

Soak the kombu in a small bowl of room temperature water until reconstituted and pliable, about 10 minutes. Remove kombu and dice into ribbons.

Place the kombu in a large saucepan. Layer the celery, onion, cabbage, carrots, corn, squash and millet on top. Add the water and broth.

Bring the soup to a boil. Reduce heat to low, cover and simmer 30 minutes.

Just before serving, mix the miso with ¼ cup of water. Stir the miso and salt into the soup.

START TO FINISH:

50 minutes

Makes 4 servings

TIP: For even greater interest, use a mix of grains. Try ⅓ cup millet, ⅓ cup short-grain brown rice and ⅓ cup wheat berries. The different grains will give the soup a great mix of tastes and textures. Increase cooking time to 45 minutes.

brazilian black bean soup

This hearty soup goes great with cornbread and greens. Don't let the long list of ingredients intimidate you. It takes only minutes to prepare the vegetables.

START TO FINISH:

35 minutes
Makes 4–6 servings

TIP: For a creamy garnish, drizzle soy sour cream in a circular pattern on top of the soup and sprinkle with diced scallions.

2	tablespoons extra-virgin olive oil
1	large green bell pepper, seeded and chopped
4	cloves garlic, minced
½	teaspoon ground cloves
1	bay leaf
2	medium onions, chopped
2	stalks celery, chopped
1	medium carrot, ends trimmed, cut into thin rounds
2	15-ounce cans black beans
3 ½	cups water
½	cup orange juice
2	ounces tempeh bacon, chopped
1	cup corn kernels
¼	cup mirin
1	tablespoon brown rice vinegar
1	teaspoon ground cumin
1	teaspoon ground coriander
1	teaspoon red pepper flakes
1	teaspoon dried oregano
1	teaspoon sea salt

Combine the oil, bell pepper, garlic, cloves, bay leaf, onions, celery and carrots in a large, deep skillet. Cook over a medium-high flame until the vegetables are just tender, about 5 minutes.

Add remaining ingredients and bring to a simmer. Reduce the heat to low, cover and simmer 15 minutes.

Discard the bay leaf. Transfer half of the soup to a blender and purée until chunky smooth, about 15 seconds. Return mixture to the skillet and stir. Simmer an additional 5 minutes.

hot-and-sour soup

The contrast of flavors makes this soup a favorite.

2 cups vegetable broth

2 cups water

¼ cup brown rice vinegar

3 tablespoons soy sauce

3 tablespoons grated fresh ginger

4 cloves garlic, minced

½ teaspoon red pepper flakes

¾ cup sliced scallions

1 red bell pepper, seeded and diced

1 cup thinly sliced shiitake mushrooms

1 cup snow peas, cut lengthwise into strips

1 cup shredded bok choy

⅔ cup extra-firm tofu, cut into ½-inch cubes

1 tablespoon arrowroot mixed with 2 tablespoons water

2 teaspoons toasted sesame seed oil

2 tablespoons minced fresh cilantro

Combine the broth, water, vinegar and soy sauce in a large saucepan. Bring to a boil over a high flame.

Add the ginger, garlic, pepper flakes and ½ cup of the scallions. Reduce the flame to low, cover and simmer 5 minutes.

Add bell pepper and cook 4 minutes. Stir in mushrooms, snow peas, bok choy and tofu. Cook, uncovered, until the snow peas are just tender, about 4 minutes.

Add the arrowroot mixture. Cook 1 minute, stirring constantly until the broth thickens. Remove from the heat and stir in sesame oil and remaining scallions.

Garnish with cilantro just before serving.

shaker bean soup

The inspiration for this soup came from versions prepared by New England's Shakers, a religious group that thrived during the 19th century.

15-ounce can pinto beans

15-ounce can baked beans

6 cups vegetable broth

½ yellow onion, diced

2 celery stalks, with leaves, chopped

1½ cups chopped tomatoes

1 tablespoon hot pepper sauce

1 teaspoon sea salt

½ teaspoon freshly ground black pepper

1 tablespoon molasses

1 tablespoon extra-virgin olive oil

2 tablespoons unbleached white flour

Combine the beans, broth, onion and celery in a large stockpot. Bring to a boil over a medium-high flame. Reduce heat, cover and simmer 30 minutes.

Add the tomato, hot pepper sauce, salt, pepper and molasses.

In a small saucepan, combine the oil and flour. Whisk over a medium flame 2–3 minutes or until lightly browned. Remove about 1 cup of broth from the soup and slowly pour into the pan of oil and flour, whisking constantly. Simmer 5 minutes or until the mixture thickens slightly. Transfer to the stockpot and stir to combine.

Simmer soup another 15 minutes.

START TO FINISH:
1 hour
Makes 4–6 servings

TIP: To make this soup especially thick, transfer half of the beans and about a third of the liquid to a blender after the initial 30 minutes of simmering. Purée until smooth, then return the mixture to the pot and continue cooking.

caldo verde

Made the traditional way, this Portuguese "green soup" calls for chorizo, a peppery sausage. We've replaced the chorizo with soy sausage. Spicy baked tofu also works.

START TO FINISH:

50 minutes
(15 minutes active)
Makes 4–6 servings

TIP: It's best to lightly brown the soy sausage or tofu in olive oil before adding it to the soup. This helps hold it together and gives it a more savory flavor.

2 tablespoons extra-virgin olive oil

1 clove garlic, minced

1 large red onion, diced

8 ounces soy sausage, cut into ¼-inch chunks

2 quarts vegetable broth

1 pound Yukon Gold potatoes, cut into ½-inch chunks

2 teaspoons sea salt

1 teaspoon freshly ground black pepper

1 pound kale, stems removed, cut into ribbons

2 tablespoons minced fresh dill

Combine the oil, garlic and onion in a large stockpot and sauté over a medium-high flame 4 minutes. Add half of the soy sausage and cook another 3–4 minutes or until the onion is soft.

Add the broth, potatoes, salt and pepper and bring the soup to a boil. Reduce the heat, cover and simmer 12–15 minutes or until the potatoes are tender.

Transfer the soup, in batches if necessary, to a blender or food processor and purée until chunky smooth. Return soup to the pot.

Add remaining ingredients and cook, uncovered, another 10 minutes over a medium flame. Serve hot.

vegetarian chili

Looking for a chili with that perfect balance of heat and sweet? Serve this by the bowl, over saffron rice or as a topping for nachos.

START TO FINISH:

50 minutes

Makes 4–6 servings

TIP: Instead of ground meat substitute (available frozen or refrigerated), try dried textured soy protein. Prepare the protein as directed (usually simmer 1:1 water and a splash of soy sauce or ketchup), then add as directed in the recipe.

3	tablespoons extra-virgin olive oil
2½	teaspoons chili powder
1	teaspoon sea salt
¾	teaspoon cinnamon
¾	teaspoon ground coriander
¾	teaspoon ground cumin
½	teaspoon crushed red pepper flakes
12	ounces ground beef substitute
1	medium red onion, diced
2	tablespoons soy sauce
2	cloves garlic, minced
	28-ounce can crushed tomatoes
1	cup water
	15-ounce can kidney beans, drained
	15-ounce can black beans, drained
1	cup corn kernels
¾	pound (1 large) sweet potato, cut into ½-inch chunks

Combine oil, chili powder, salt, cinnamon, coriander, cumin and red pepper flakes in a large saucepan over a medium-high flame. Cook 2 minutes, stirring constantly, until spices are fragrant.

Add the ground beef substitute, onion and soy sauce, and sauté, stirring frequently, until onions are soft, about 6 minutes.

Stir in remaining ingredients. Cover and simmer 30 minutes or until sweet potatoes are tender. Stir occasionally.

berry good chili

When it comes to chili, it doesn't get much better than this tangy, sweet-and-spicy red-hot recipe. Serve with nacho chips or freshly baked flatbread.

START TO FINISH:
1 hour
Makes 4–6 servings

1	medium yellow onion, diced
1	red bell pepper, seeded and diced
1	green bell pepper, seeded and diced
1	cup corn kernels
1½	cups long-grain white rice
1	cup tomato paste
1½	cups fresh or frozen cranberries
½	cup unsweetened dried cherries
	15-ounce can navy beans *or* other white beans
	15-ounce can kidney beans
2	teaspoons chili powder
1	teaspoon paprika
1	teaspoon crushed red pepper flakes
⅓	cup maple syrup
1	teaspoon sea salt
1	teaspoon yellow mustard powder
6 ½	cups vegetable broth

TIP: If you have cooked rice on hand, this recipe can be made in just 15 minutes. If so, use 2 cups of cooked rice and only 3½ cups of vegetable broth.

Dried, unsweetened cranberries can be substituted for fresh or frozen. Use 1 cup of dried cranberries and an additional ½ cup of broth.

Combine all ingredients in a large stockpot. Bring to a simmer, cover and cook 1 hour or until rice is tender and liquid has reduced by about a third.

vegetables

sweet winter squash with fresh thyme

Bring new life to an old side dish with this simple preparation. Rather than the usual steam and mash, this recipe calls for sautéing butternut squash and onions, then slowly simmering in white wine. As the wine reduces, it gives the squash a distinct, but not distracting, sweetness.

3 tablespoons extra-virgin olive oil

1 small butternut squash, peeled, seeded and cut into thin matchsticks (about 1¼ pounds, or 5 cups)

2 medium onions, diced

4–5 sprigs fresh thyme or ½ teaspoon dried thyme

½ teaspoon sea salt

½ teaspoon freshly ground black pepper

2 cups sweet white wine, such as Riesling

Combine the oil, squash, onions and thyme in a large skillet and sauté over a high flame until onions are just tender, about 6 minutes.

Season with salt and pepper. Add wine and cook for 1 minute. Cover and reduce heat to medium. Cook until squash is tender, about 30 minutes.

Remove the cover and cook until liquid has mostly reduced, about 10 minutes. Adjust salt and pepper if needed.

START TO FINISH:
50 minutes
Makes 4 servings

TIP: Add ½ teaspoon red pepper flakes to complement the sweet with a bit of heat. To make this a one-dish meal, add cubed seitan or tofu during the final 5 minutes.

southwest bean and corn cakes

Top these hearty, spicy patties with a fiery salsa.

START TO FINISH:

40 minutes

Makes 6–8 cakes

TIP: Just about any patty or croquette that calls for pan frying in oil can be baked to cut down on fat. Place the patties on a lightly oiled baking sheet and bake at 400°F about 30 minutes or until the patties are crisp.

1½	cups corn kernels
1	cup cornmeal
½	cup whole wheat pastry flour
1½	teaspoons baking powder
1	teaspoon ground cumin
1	teaspoon sea salt
1	teaspoon red pepper flakes
1	tablespoon lime juice
	Pinch cayenne pepper
¼	teaspoon freshly ground black pepper
1	teaspoon paprika
	15-ounce can black beans
1	medium yellow onion, diced
1	medium carrot, finely grated
1¾	cups plain rice milk
2	teaspoons cider vinegar

Preheat the oven to 350°F. Lightly oil a baking sheet.

In a large bowl, combine the corn kernels, cornmeal, flour, baking powder, cumin, salt, red pepper flakes, lime juice, cayenne pepper, black pepper and paprika. Mix well.

In a separate bowl, use a potato masher to coarsely mash the beans. Add the onion and carrot and mix to form a thick mixture.

Add the rice milk and vinegar to the beans and mix to combine. Add the bean and rice milk mixture to the corn mixture and mix together.

Use your hands to scoop some of the dough to make burger-size patties. Arrange patties on the baking sheet and bake 15 minutes. Flip the patties and bake another 15 minutes or until crisp around the edges.

pita (spanakopita)

This recipe has been a family favorite for years. When we first started making it, we followed the Greek tradition and loaded on the butter and feta and cottage cheeses. That was fine in our hefty and not-so-healthy days, but no more.

With a bit of tinkering, we created a version that retained the flavor and cheesy satisfaction but vastly reduced the fat and eliminated the dairy.

The dilemma is knowing when to eat it. Our tradition is to serve it warm at dinner, and a few hours later raid the refrigerator for cold leftovers.

The recipe may seem intricate, but it speeds along and the result is well worth the effort.

COTTAGE "CHEESE":

- 1 pound extra-firm tofu, drained and mashed
- ¾ cup tofu mayonnaise
- 3 teaspoons finely minced onion
- 4 cloves garlic, minced
- 1 teaspoon sea salt
- 1 teaspoon ground dill seed

FETA "CHEESE":

- 1 pound extra-firm tofu, drained and cut into ¼-inch cubes
- 2 cups water
- 3 tablespoons nutritional yeast flakes
- 1 teaspoon sea salt
- 2 teaspoons finely minced onion
- 2 cloves garlic, minced
- ½ teaspoon ground cumin
- ½ teaspoon dried thyme
- ½ teaspoon dried marjoram
- ½ teaspoon ground dill seed

FETA "CHEESE" MARINADE:

- ¼ cup red wine vinegar
- ¼ cup water

START TO FINISH:

90 minutes (not counting "cheese" making) Makes 12 servings

TIP: While working with filo dough, keep the unused portions covered with a damp towel. This keeps the sheets from drying and becoming brittle. Be sure to thaw filo in the refrigerator overnight; thawing at room temperature makes it mushy.

Prepare the "cheeses" a few days before to speed up this recipe. The cheese substitutes were inspired by recipes from Joanne Stepaniak's wonderful *The Uncheese Cookbook*, a great resource if you want the taste of cheese minus the dairy.

This recipe calls for kale and spinach (traditional spanakopita uses only spinach). Using all of one or the other works fine, too.

2 tablespoons tahini

2 tablespoons fresh lemon juice

1 teaspoon sea salt

1 teaspoon dried basil

1 teaspoon dried oregano

½ teaspoon finely minced garlic

PITA:

1-pound package frozen filo dough (any variety will work)

¾ pound kale

¾ pound spinach leaves

2 large yellow onions, diced

1 tablespoon extra-virgin olive oil

1 teaspoon sea salt

1½ teaspoons dill seed

Olive oil in a spray bottle for spraying layers of filo

Start by making the soy cottage cheese. Place all ingredients in a large bowl and mix thoroughly. Don't use a food processor or the soy cheese will be too smooth. Set aside.

To make the soy feta cheese, combine all ingredients in a saucepan. Bring the mixture to a boil over a medium-high flame, then simmer 20 minutes, stirring occasionally. Drain the tofu and set aside in a bowl.

To make the marinade for the soy feta, whisk all ingredients together in a bowl. Pour the marinade over the feta and toss to coat. Cover and chill several hours, stirring occasionally. Once marinated, the soy feta can be refrigerated up to 1 week. Discard the marinade before using the feta.

To assemble the pita, preheat the oven to 350°F. Remove the filo dough from its package and cover with a damp cloth. Remove the stems from the kale and spinach and discard. Finely chop the leaves.

In a medium skillet, cook the onion in the oil until translucent, about 6 minutes.

Crumble the soy feta into a large bowl and mix in the soy cottage cheese. Add the onions, salt, dill seeds, kale and spinach. Mix well (hands work best).

Lightly brush the bottom of a lasagna pan with oil. Place a layer of filo dough (2 or 3 sheets) on the bottom of the pan, curling the excess up the sides.

Lightly spray the filo with oil and spread a ¼- to ½-inch layer of kale and tofu filling over it. Cover the mixture with another layer of filo dough, again layering any excess dough up the sides of the pan. Lightly spray with oil, and repeat until all of kale and tofu mixture has been used or the top of the pan is reached.

Top the pita with a final layer of filo. Lightly spray the filo with oil. Bake 45 minutes or until the top of the filo is lightly browned.

mémère's shepherd's pie

Our great-grandmother used to make an unhealthy but oh-so-tasty version of this heavenly dish. This version retains the rich textures and meatiness of the original but lacks the beef and dairy.

PIE:

- 3 large boiling potatoes, unpeeled, cut into ½-inch chunks
- 2 tablespoons sesame oil
- 2 medium onions, diced
- 1½ cups diced white button mushrooms
- 1 pound seitan, cut into ½-inch chunks
- 2 tablespoons soy sauce
- 1 cup plain rice milk
- 2 tablespoons soy margarine
- 2 cups corn kernels

GRAVY:

- 2 tablespoons toasted sesame seed oil
- 1 cup diced shiitake mushrooms
- 2 scallions, diced
- ¼ cup soy sauce
- 1¼ cups water
- 1 tablespoon kuzu

Preheat the oven to 350°F. Place the potatoes in a medium saucepan and cover with water. Bring to a boil over a medium flame and cook 12–15 minutes or until the potatoes are easily pierced with a fork. Drain and set aside.

Meanwhile, in a large skillet, heat the sesame oil over a medium flame and sauté the onions and button mushrooms until the onions are translucent, about 6 minutes. Add the seitan and soy sauce. Cook another 2–3 minutes and set aside.

In a medium bowl, use a potato masher or heavy whisk to whip the potatoes, rice milk and soy margarine.

Spread the onion and seitan mixture evenly over the bottom of a glass or stainless steel loaf pan. Spread the corn kernels over the mixture. Spread

START TO FINISH:

1 hour

Makes 4–6 servings

TIP: To make this extra-savory, add ¼ cup of nutritional yeast flakes to the onions.

the mashed potatoes over the corn. Cover the dish with foil and bake 25–30 minutes. Uncover during the last 5–10 minutes to let potatoes brown.

Toward the end of the baking, combine all gravy ingredients except water and kuzu in a small saucepan. Sauté over a medium flame about 3 minutes. Add 1 cup water and simmer over low flame 5 minutes.

In a small glass, combine kuzu and remaining water. Add to gravy and stir until it thickens.

To serve, pour gravy over each helping of pie.

baked breaded eggplant with sweet tomato sauce

Breaded eggplant is delicious. But usually it is coated with egg, fried and then slathered with melted cheese. This version removes the animal products and significantly reduces the fat.

	12-ounce package soft, silken tofu
6	tablespoons extra-virgin olive oil
3	cups dry seasoned breadcrumbs
1	large eggplant, peeled and sliced into ⅓-inch-thick rounds
1	medium yellow onion, diced
2	pounds tomatoes, coarsely chopped, with juices
1	tablespoon hot pepper sauce
⅓	cup maple syrup
1	teaspoon sea salt
1	teaspoon freshly ground black pepper
½	teaspoon celery seed

Preheat the oven to 400°F. Combine the tofu and 2 tablespoons oil in a blender or food processor and purée until smooth. Transfer the mixture to a wide, shallow bowl. Pour the breadcrumbs into a similar bowl.

Use another 2 tablespoons of oil to liberally coat a baking sheet.

Dredge the eggplant slices through the tofu mixture so that both sides are lightly coated. One at a time, set each slice in the bowl of breadcrumbs, first on one side, then on the other, to cover the slice completely. Shake off extra crumbs. Place the eggplant slices on the baking sheet.

Bake 45 minutes or until crispy and just beginning to brown.

Meanwhile, make the sauce by combining the remaining oil and the diced onion in a deep skillet. Sauté over a medium-high flame 6 minutes or until onion becomes translucent.

Add remaining ingredients and simmer 15 minutes.

To serve, place two or three slices of eggplant on a plate and top generously with sauce. Sprinkle soy Parmesan on top, if desired.

START TO FINISH:
1 hour
Makes 4 servings

TIP: The easiest way to peel an eggplant is to cut off the ends so it can stand upright. Then use a paring knife or peeler to carefully cut the skin away from the flesh.

To prevent raw eggplant slices from browning while you work, keep them in a bowl of lightly salted water. You may need a small plate to weigh them down under the water.

curry butternut squash

Partner the creamy sweetness of butternut squash with the exotic flavor of curry for a winning combination.

START TO FINISH:
25 minutes
Makes 4 servings

TIP: You can substitute corn oil for the olive oil to add a buttery flavor. Squash varies in water content. As it cooks, check to ensure it isn't sticking. Add water if necessary.

2 tablespoons extra-virgin olive oil

1 medium yellow onion, diced

1 medium red bell pepper, seeded and diced

1 medium green bell pepper, seeded and diced

3 medium garlic cloves, minced

1 teaspoon curry powder

2 pounds butternut squash, peeled, seeded and cut into small cubes

¼ cup water

   Pinch of sea salt

1 tablespoon minced fresh cilantro

Combine the oil, onion and bell peppers in a large skillet and sauté over a medium-high flame 3 minutes.

Stir in garlic and curry powder and cook 1 minute. Stir in squash, water, salt and cilantro. Cover and cook over a medium-low flame until squash is tender, about 15 minutes. To serve, leave the squash chunky or mash.

sesame steamed green beans

START TO FINISH:

25 minutes

Makes 4 servings

TIP: Toasted sesame oil can be a pain to work with. Once opened, the bottle needs to be refrigerated. But sesame oil hardens when refrigerated, making it difficult to use straight from the refrigerator. To speed things up, make sure the lid is tight, then set the bottle in a bowl or sink of warm water 3–4 minutes.

Here is a great way to dress up green beans with little effort. A quick steam followed by a dousing of toasted sesame seed oil and a shake of sesame seeds is all it takes to transform something plain into something perfect.

3	**tablespoons sesame seeds**
1	**pound fresh green beans**
¼	**cup toasted sesame seed oil**
1	**tablespoon maple syrup**
1	**teaspoon red wine vinegar**

Place the sesame seeds in a small, heavy skillet and heat over a medium flame. Toast the seeds until they are dry and just begin to brown, about 5 minutes. Seeds will begin to pop when done. Transfer to a small bowl and set aside.

Bring about 1 inch of water to a boil in a saucepan fitted with a steamer basket. Snip off the ends of the beans and cut into 2-inch lengths.

Place the beans in the steamer basket. Cover and steam 5 minutes or until the beans are just tender.

While the beans steam, whisk together the sesame seed oil, maple syrup and vinegar in a medium saucepan and bring to a simmer. Set aside.

Transfer the beans to the saucepan containing the sesame oil mixture. Toss the beans to coat.

Transfer the beans to a serving dish and spoon pan liquid over them. Sprinkle with toasted sesame seeds.

italian spinach

This is a great way to serve spinach or any leafy greens. The wonderful tangy flavor of this spinach will appeal even to those who usually pass on greens.

4   tablespoons golden raisins

2   tablespoons extra-virgin olive oil

1   tablespoon fresh rosemary leaves

1   tablespoon fresh thyme

5   tablespoons capers

4   tablespoons pine nuts

    Pinch nutmeg

1   teaspoon curry powder

4   pounds fresh spinach (or other dark leafy greens, such as kale or chard)

    Sea salt and freshly ground black pepper, to taste

Place the raisins in a small bowl and cover with warm water. Soak 20 minutes then drain and set aside.

Meanwhile, combine the oil, rosemary and thyme in a large, deep skillet. Heat over a medium-high flame.

Add the capers and use the back of a large fork to roughly crush them. Stir to combine with other ingredients.

Add the pine nuts, nutmeg and curry powder and stir.

Chop the thick stems off the spinach leaves and discard. Wash the spinach and, without removing excess water from the leaves, add them and the raisins to the skillet.

Sauté the spinach 2–3 minutes or until wilted. Stir frequently to coat with the seasonings and oil. Season with salt and pepper to taste.

START TO FINISH:

20 minutes

Makes 4 servings

TIP: Don't be afraid to add to this dish. Try carrots chopped into matchsticks, diced red pepper or any other brightly colored vegetable. Jicama also is nice.

seasoned roasted vegetables

Roasting vegetables adds a sweetness unmatched by other cooking methods. Vary the types of vegetables according to the season.

START TO FINISH:

50 minutes

Makes 6–8 servings

TIP: Cut the vegetables to similar sizes so they finish cooking at the same time.

Leftover roasted vegetables are great to toss into a soup.

1 pound Yukon Gold potatoes (or other baking potatoes), unpeeled, cut into ½-inch chunks

3 carrots, ends trimmed, cut into ½-inch rounds

2 parsnips, cut into ½-inch chunks

12 Brussels sprouts, cut in half lengthwise

1 turnip, cut into ½-inch chunks

1 medium sweet potato, unpeeled, cut into ½-inch chunks

1 rutabaga, cut into ½-inch chunks

2 onions, cut into wedges

6 tablespoons extra-virgin olive oil

4 cloves garlic, crushed

1 teaspoon dried oregano

1 teaspoon dried basil

1 teaspoon fresh rosemary

1 teaspoon dried thyme

1 teaspoon sea salt

Sea salt and freshly ground black pepper, to taste

Preheat the oven to 425°F. Place the vegetables in a large bowl.

In a small bowl, whisk together the oil, garlic and seasonings. Pour the marinade over the vegetables and toss well to coat evenly. Let stand 5 minutes.

Transfer the vegetables and marinade to a baking sheet with sides. Roast 15 minutes, then turn the vegetables. Roast another 15 minutes, then turn again and cook 10 minutes more.

Vegetables should be tender and caramelized. Season with salt and pepper immediately.

maple-glazed carrots

Here's a cold weather favorite, especially around the holidays. It's a great way to get picky eaters to dig into their vegetables.

START TO FINISH:

30 minutes

Makes 4 servings

TIP: The sauce can be made ahead of time. Combine the sauce ingredients in a small saucepan and heat over a medium-high flame 3–5 minutes or until thick. Refrigerate until needed. When reheating, simmer but don't boil.

 2 tablespoons toasted sesame seed oil

 12 medium carrots (about 2 pounds), cut into ½-inch rounds

SAUCE:

 ½ cup water *or* vegetable broth

 ¼ cup maple syrup

 3 tablespoons ketchup

 1 tablespoon kuzu, mixed with 3 tablespoons water

 ½ teaspoon paprika

 Pinch sea salt

Combine the oil and carrots in a large skillet and sauté over a medium flame about 4 minutes, stirring frequently.

Whisk together the remaining ingredients in a small bowl. Add to the carrots. Cover and reduce heat to low. Simmer 15 minutes or until the carrots are tender and easily pierced with a fork.

Remove the cover and check the liquid. If it is thin and runs easily off the carrots, continue simmering 3–5 minutes to thicken the sauce.

To serve, transfer the carrots to a bowl and spoon sauce over the top.

maple-curried carrots

*Variants of these warmly spiced carrots are served as an appetizer in Portugal.
They usually are accompanied by fresh, warm bread, olive oil and a bowl of olives.
The Portuguese serve them room temperature, but they also are good warm.*

START TO FINISH:
15 minutes
Makes 4–6 servings

1	pound carrots, ends trimmed, cut into small chunks
1½	cups sweet white wine
2	teaspoons red curry paste
1	teaspoon dry sage
⅛	teaspoon nutmeg
¼	teaspoon cinnamon
3	tablespoons maple syrup
1	6-ounce can tomato paste

Combine all ingredients except the tomato paste in a medium saucepan.
Cover and bring to a simmer over a medium-high flame. Cook 5 minutes.

Uncover and cook another 5 minutes or until the liquid has mostly reduced.
Stir in the tomato paste and cook another 2 minutes or until warm.

TIP: Visit an Asian market for a wonderful selection of curry pastes. Try stirring a teaspoon or two into rice just as it finishes cooking. Or blend with soy sauce and maple syrup and use to coat still hot dry-roasted almonds and cashews.

maple-gingered corn

Here's a perfect Thanksgiving side dish. Light, refreshing sweet corn offers an alternative to the heavier dishes usually found at the holiday table. Of course it's nice to use fresh corn cut from the cob, but frozen kernels work fine.

2	tablespoons corn oil
½	teaspoon ground cumin
1½	teaspoons grated fresh ginger
2	medium tomatoes, coarsely chopped
¾	cup finely diced onion
½	teaspoon sea salt
2	tablespoons maple syrup
4	cups corn kernels

Heat the oil in a large skillet over a medium flame. Add the cumin and ginger and sauté 1 minute, stirring constantly. Add the tomatoes, onions and salt and bring to a simmer. Cook about 4 minutes or until nearly dry.

Add the maple syrup and corn and return to a simmer. Cook 10 minutes, stirring frequently, until the corn is heated through.

START TO FINISH:

20 minutes

Makes 4 servings

TIP: Olive oil doesn't work well in this recipe. Its strong flavor competes with the mellow taste of corn. If you do not have corn oil, try canola, which has a mild flavor.

sesame ginger-steamed vegetables

Steamed vegetables get oomph with this warm and savory sauce.

START TO FINISH:
20 minutes
Makes 4 servings

TIP: For a sauce with more body, add a 2-ounce piece of soft silken tofu while puréeing.

- 4 medium carrots, ends trimmed, cut into 1-inch chunks
- 3 cups broccoli florets
- ½ pound green beans
- 1 clove garlic, peeled
- 1-inch piece fresh ginger
- 1½ tablespoons sweet white miso
- 1 cup vegetable broth
- 1 teaspoon toasted sesame seed oil
- 2 teaspoons lightly toasted sesame seeds

Bring 1 inch of water to a boil in a large saucepan fitted with a steamer basket. Place the carrots, broccoli and green beans in the basket. Cover and steam until the carrots are tender, about 5 minutes. Set aside.

Combine the remaining ingredients, except 1 teaspoon of sesame seeds, in a blender or food processor and purée until smooth.

Arrange the vegetables in a serving bowl. Drizzle with sauce and sprinkle remaining sesame seeds over the top.

tropical sweet potatoes

This is a healthy twist on the traditional candied yams or sugar-drenched sweet potatoes that appear at Thanksgiving. This version is just as good, but its mild sweetness is easier on the palate and won't overwhelm the other foods on your plate.

START TO FINISH:

1 hour, 40 minutes (20 minutes active)

Makes 6 servings

TIP: Though this should be baked no more than a few hours before serving, some preparation can be done well in advance. Bake, peel and slice the potatoes the night before. The banana purée also can be made ahead of time—the acid in the orange juice will keep the bananas from turning brown. Be sure to keep the purée refrigerated until used.

2–3 medium sweet potatoes
1 tablespoon corn oil
2 medium bananas
¾ cup orange juice
¼ cup maple syrup
½ teaspoon sea salt
½ tablespoon kuzu
¼ cup chopped pecans
½ cup cashew pieces
¼ cup flaked coconut

Preheat the oven to 400°F. Pierce each sweet potato several times with a fork. Wrap in foil and bake 45–50 minutes or until tender.

Remove the sweet potatoes from the oven and cool. Leave the oven on. Peel the sweet potatoes and slice into thin rounds.

Coat a 2-quart casserole dish with the oil. Layer the sweet potato slices in the baking dish.

Combine the bananas, orange juice, maple syrup, salt and kuzu in a blender. Process until smooth. Drizzle the mixture over the sweet potatoes.

Sprinkle with pecans and cashews. Top with the coconut.

Cover the dish and bake 15 minutes. Uncover and bake an additional 15 minutes. Cool 10 minutes before serving.

sweet apricot potatoes with pine nuts

Oven-roasted potatoes usually are hot and spicy, or sprinkled with Italian herbs. We decided it was time to give potatoes a sweet treatment.

1½	pounds new *or* small red potatoes, unpeeled, cut into ½-inch chunks
2	tablespoons extra-virgin olive oil
3	tablespoons all-fruit apricot jam
3	tablespoons water
1	teaspoon sea salt
¼	cup chopped fresh dill
⅓	cup pine nuts

Preheat the oven to 400°F.

Combine the potatoes and oil in a large bowl and toss to coat evenly. Spread the potatoes in a 9 × 9-inch baking dish.

In a medium bowl, whisk together the jam, water, salt and dill. Alternatively, process in a blender, adding the dill after the machine is shut off.

Pour the mixture over the potatoes and toss to coat. Sprinkle with pine nuts. Cover the baking dish with foil and bake 45 minutes or until the potatoes are tender.

Remove the foil during the final 10 minutes of baking. During final 2 minutes, increase heat to broil to lightly brown the potatoes.

Before serving, toss the potatoes to coat with the sauce in the baking dish. Season lightly with salt.

START TO FINISH:
1 hour
(10 minutes active)
Makes 4 servings

TIP: For more of a sweet-and-sour flavor, add 1 tablespoon balsamic vinegar to the jam mixture.

tuscan-baked veggie potatoes

This recipe was born out of desperation. We were in Tuscany and had misjudged how early Italian markets close on Sunday afternoons.

After much searching, we found a vegetable stand and bought whatever was fresh, and a bottle of the local white wine, of course.

This simple, easy dish is the surprising result. We couldn't believe how good it was or how rich just a few vegetables could be. Accompany this with a dry white wine.

START TO FINISH:
50 minutes
Makes 4 servings

TIP: When you don't have fresh herbs, soak dried ones in several tablespoons of olive oil about 1 hour before using. Never store oil containing herbs in the cupboard; this breeds botulism.

- 4 medium baking potatoes, unpeeled, cut into ½-inch chunks
- 3 tablespoons extra-virgin olive oil, plus ¼ cup
- 3 tablespoons fresh rosemary leaves
- 3 tablespoons fresh lavender leaves
- 2 small onions, diced into medium chunks
- 1 large red bell pepper, cut to a ½-inch dice
- 1 cup dry white wine
- 4 medium tomatoes, roughly diced
- 1 medium eggplant, peeled and cubed
- 1 cup breadcrumbs

Preheat the oven to 350°F. In a large bowl, toss the potatoes, 3 tablespoons oil, rosemary and lavender until the potatoes are coated.

Transfer potatoes to a 9 × 9-inch baking dish. Scrape as much oil from the bowl into the baking dish as possible. Bake until potatoes are tender on the inside and crisp on the outside, about 20 minutes.

Meanwhile, combine the onion, pepper and wine in a large, deep skillet. Simmer until the vegetables are just tender, 5–7 minutes.

Add the tomatoes and eggplant and simmer until the eggplant is tender and the tomatoes have broken down into a sauce, about 12 minutes.

Remove the baking dish from the oven and spread the tomato and eggplant mixture over the potatoes. Top with breadcrumbs and drizzle with remaining oil. Bake an additional 10 minutes or until the breadcrumbs begin to brown.

Remove from the oven and let stand 10 minutes before serving.

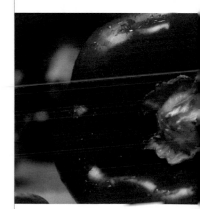

wasabi-ginger mashed potatoes

START TO FINISH:

25 minutes

Makes 4 servings

TIP: Wasabi powder is a great way to add zip to just about any dish. Add ½ teaspoon to the oil when stir-frying rice and vegetables.

Add an Asian zip to an all-American favorite. The combination of wasabi and ginger livens up this dish without overpowering the creamy goodness we love.

Don't worry about missing the butter. The corn oil provides the dish with a similar flavor. We prefer to steam our potatoes and to leave the skins on them.

- 2 **pounds boiling potatoes, unpeeled, cut into 1-inch chunks**
- 1 **tablespoon sea salt**
- 1½ **teaspoons freshly grated ginger**
- 1 **cup plain soy yogurt**
- 2 **tablespoons corn oil *or* soy margarine**
- 1 **tablespoon chopped fresh dill**
- 1 **tablespoon wasabi powder**

Bring about 2 inches of water to a boil in a large saucepan fitted with a steamer basket. Place the potatoes in the basket and steam until they are easily pierced with a fork, about 15 minutes.

Transfer the potatoes to a large bowl. Mash the potatoes, adding remaining ingredients.

baked sweet potato wedges

>   2 tablespoons extra-virgin olive oil
>   2 teaspoons chili powder
>   ½ teaspoon dried thyme
>   ½ teaspoon freshly ground black pepper
>   ¼ teaspoon paprika
>   2 pounds sweet potatoes, unpeeled, cut into ½-inch wedges
>   Kosher salt *or* coarse sea salt

Preheat the oven to 425°F. Lightly oil a baking sheet.

In a large bowl or plastic bag, combine all remaining ingredients except the sweet potatoes and salt. Add the sweet potatoes and either toss or shake to coat.

Spread the sweet potatoes on the baking sheet. Season lightly with salt and bake 40 minutes, turning once, until browned and crisp. Salt to taste, if needed.

START TO FINISH:

50 minutes

Makes 4 servings

TIP: For a spicier version, add ½ teaspoon each of ground cumin and cayenne pepper to the oil for coating the sweet potatoes. Russet, white or red potatoes can be substituted.

tofu à la king

Here is a creamy, meaty favorite perfect for brunch, lunch or dinner. Try it ladled over Fluffy Biscuits (recipe p. 34) or oversized slices of fresh sourdough bread, lightly toasted and drizzled with olive oil. It also is wonderful served in bread bowls or baked into a pastry shell as a pot pie filling.

START TO FINISH:
30 minutes
Makes 4 servings

TIP: For variety, substitute seitan for the tofu.

      2 **tablespoons extra-virgin olive oil**

      4 **cups sliced white button mushrooms**

    ½ **small yellow onion, chopped**

      1 **green bell pepper, seeded and chopped**

      4 **tablespoons whole wheat flour**

3 ¼ **cups soy milk**

      1 **pound extra-firm tofu, cut into cubes**

    ½ **cup frozen green peas**

        Sea salt and freshly ground black pepper, to taste

        Pinch paprika

Combine the oil, mushrooms, onion and green pepper in a deep skillet and sauté over a medium-high flame until the vegetables are tender, about 5 minutes.

Stir in the flour and cook 2 minutes, stirring constantly. Gradually add the soy milk. Bring the mixture to a boil while continuing to stir until thickened.

Add the tofu, peas, salt, pepper and paprika. Reduce heat to low and simmer 5 minutes.

pasta and noodles

homemade pasta

There is no substitute for fresh homemade pasta. And it is so simple, enough to feed four can be made in the time it takes to boil the water in which it will be cooked.

This egg-free recipe originates in the south of Italy, where traditional pastas call for only semolina flour and water.

2 **cups semolina flour, plus additional for kneading**

Water

Set a large stockpot of lightly salted water over a high flame and bring to a boil.

Place the flour in a large bowl. Add ⅓ cup of water and begin incorporating it with a fork. Work in the water even though it will not appear to be enough. Add water, 1 tablespoon at a time, until the flour has mostly clumped together but still is relatively dry. Push the dough together and turn out onto a work surface lightly dusted with additional flour.

Knead the dough, pushing it away from your body and folding it over on itself. Knead about 5 minutes, adding additional flour to the work surface as needed to prevent sticking. The dough is ready when it is smooth and looks and feels like skin.

Roll the dough into a thick log 6–8 inches long. Cut the log into 1-inch pieces. Cover all but one piece with a damp cloth to prevent drying. Roll the piece into a long strand about ½ inch thick and 10 inches long.

Cut the strand into ½-inch segments. Using either a gnocchi board or the back of a fork, roll each segment over the ridges of the board or the prongs of the fork to flatten and create ridges in the pasta. The finished pasta should be round to oblong, thinner in the middle than on the edges and grooved on one side.

Set the finished pasta on a platter lightly dusted with semolina flour. Repeat with remaining dough.

When all the pasta has been prepared, cook it in boiling water until the pieces float, about 4 minutes. Drain and serve.

START TO FINISH:

20 minutes

Makes 4 servings

TIP: These directions explain how to make orecchiette pasta, which resembles tiny ear lobes. The dough can be used for nearly any pasta variety. Roll it out in sheets for lasagna. Or cut the sheets into squares for ravioli.

A gnocchi board is a handy tool for making this and other small pastas, including gnocchi. The wooden blocks with ridges can be purchased online.

When preparing pasta for more than four people, use a standing mixer or food processor for the initial mixing and kneading. Final kneading must be done by hand in order to feel when the dough is finished.

Semolina flour is widely available at Italian and Greek markets, as well as many natural food stores.

As with bread, water measurements when making pasta are approximate, varying depending on flour, humidity and a host of other factors. This dough should be pliable and smooth but not sticky.

bowtie pasta with vegetable ragu

A ragu is a thick, hearty sauce made from chopped vegetables and broth. Don't limit yourself to the vegetables listed here—use whatever is seasonal. Our version gets a sweet touch from fruit.

START TO FINISH:

1 hour

Makes 4 servings

TIP: Eggplant is a thirsty vegetable; it will absorb as much oil as you give it. If you are watching fat, use only 1 tablespoon of oil in the pan when baking the eggplant.

1	large eggplant
⅓	cup extra-virgin olive oil
2	pounds very ripe tomatoes
⅓	cup dried cranberries
2	red bell peppers
1	large red onion
3	medium apples
2	tablespoons capers
1	cup pitted Kalamata olives
3	tablespoons balsamic vinegar
1	cup sweet white wine (Riesling is good)
1	teaspoon sea salt
1	teaspoon freshly ground black pepper
2	cloves garlic, minced
	15-ounce can chickpeas
¾	pound bowtie (farfalle) pasta

Preheat the oven to 400°F. Cut the top off the eggplant, then slice it in half lengthwise.

Pour half the oil into the bottom of a large glass baking dish. Lay both halves of the eggplant in the baking dish, cut sides down. Bake 20 minutes or until the flesh is soft and the skin begins to wrinkle. Remove from the oven and set aside to cool.

Meanwhile, chop the tomatoes and place in a large, deep skillet with the remaining olive oil. Toss to coat. Add the cranberries and toss to combine. Roughly chop the peppers, onion and apples and add to the tomatoes. Add the capers, olives, vinegar and wine. Move the skillet to the stove and bring to a simmer over a medium-high flame. Simmer 15 minutes or until the apples are tender but not breaking apart. During the final 5 minutes of simmering add the salt, pepper, garlic and chickpeas.

While the sauce simmers, bring a large stockpot of water to a boil and cook the pasta until tender, about 8 minutes. Drain and set aside.

Toward the end of simmering, scoop the meat of the eggplant into the skillet with the tomato mixture and stir to combine.

Arrange the pasta in a serving bowl and ladle the ragu over it.

linguini with spicy caper mushroom sauce

This is a cross between a mushroom pâté and a sauté. The sauce also is good spread on thin toasts for a mushroom crostini.

4	tablespoons capers
3	tablespoons extra-virgin olive oil
½	teaspoon freshly ground black pepper
1½	teaspoons red pepper flakes
1	pound Portobello mushrooms, diced
½	cup dry white wine
¾	pound linguini pasta

Combine the capers, oil, pepper and red pepper flakes in a large, deep skillet. Heat over a medium flame 4 minutes to combine flavors. Use a fork or stiff spatula to mash the capers into the oil.

Add the mushrooms and toss to coat with oil. Reduce the flame to low and add the wine. Simmer until thick, about 10 minutes.

While the mushroom sauce simmers, bring a large stockpot of water to a boil and cook pasta until tender, about 8 minutes. Drain and set aside.

To serve, ladle the sauce over the linguini.

START TO FINISH:
30 minutes
Makes 4 servings

TIP: Just about any mushroom works in this recipe, but we like Portobello because of its meaty texture.

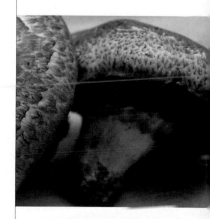

tuscan eggplant-stuffed shells

These stuffed shells can be made as quickly or slowly as you like. For the speedy version, use a prepared pasta sauce. If you have the time, use the Vegetable Ragu (recipe p. 111); it complements the dish and holds true to the Tuscan standard that fresher is better.

1	medium eggplant
16–20	pasta shells, stuffing size
1	pound extra-firm tofu
¼	cup capers
¼	cup finely diced pitted Kalamata olives
2	tablespoons minced fresh rosemary leaves
2	tablespoons minced fresh lavender leaves
1	tablespoon fresh thyme
5	sun-dried tomatoes, diced
1	teaspoon sea salt
1	tablespoon extra-virgin olive oil
2	cups tomato pasta sauce

Preheat the oven to 400°F. Slice the eggplant in half lengthwise and place the halves cut sides down in a lightly oiled baking dish. Bake until the flesh is soft and the skin is wrinkled, about 20 minutes. When done, remove from the oven and cool.

Meanwhile, bring a large stockpot of water to a boil. Cook the shells until al dente, 6–8 minutes. Drain and rinse with cool water. Set aside.

Scoop the eggplant flesh into a large bowl. Crumble the tofu into the bowl, then add remaining ingredients except the oil and pasta sauce. Mix well.

Coat a 9 × 9-inch baking dish with oil. Fill each shell with about 2 tablespoons of eggplant mixture. Arrange the shells, filling sides up, in the baking dish. Pour the sauce over the tops of the shells, allowing some to dribble into the dish. Cover with foil and bake 20 minutes. Uncover during the final 5 minutes.

START TO FINISH:
1 hour
Makes 4 servings

TIP: The shells can be boiled and stuffed ahead of time and then frozen, needing only to be thawed, sauced and baked.

pasta spirals with creamy potato and artichoke sauce

START TO FINISH:

30 minutes

Makes 4 servings

TIP: To give this sauce a fluffier texture, use a standing or hand-held mixer to whip air into it just before serving. Try the sauce with cooked rice for a quick risotto-like dish.

When choosing bottled or canned artichoke hearts for this recipe, be aware that most grocers offer two varieties: marinated in brine and packed in oil. Oil-packed artichokes can be used as is; brined artichokes should be rinsed first.

1 pound new potatoes

14-ounce can artichoke hearts

1 cup sweet white wine (Riesling works well)

¼ cup apple cider vinegar

1 tablespoon extra-virgin olive oil

1 medium yellow onion, diced

8 ounces spiral (fusilli) pasta

¾ cup vegetable broth

Sea salt and freshly ground black pepper, to taste

Bring a large stockpot of water to a boil. Wash the potatoes and cut them into quarters. Boil the potatoes until tender and easily pierced with a fork, about 20 minutes.

Meanwhile, combine the artichokes, wine, vinegar, olive oil and onion in a saucepan and bring to a simmer over a medium flame. Cook until nearly all the liquid has evaporated, about 12 minutes.

While the potatoes and artichokes cook, bring a large stockpot of lightly salted water to a boil and cook pasta until tender, about 8 minutes. Drain and set aside.

Drain the potatoes and transfer to the bowl of a food processor. Add the artichoke mixture, along with any liquid remaining in the saucepan. While slowly adding the broth, pulse until chunky smooth. Season with salt and pepper to taste.

To serve, ladle the sauce over the pasta.

pasta caponata

This classic Sicilian dish plays up the wonderful taste of capers in a hearty vegetable sauce. Capers are pickled flower buds with a tangy taste that is a cross between a pickle and an olive.

START TO FINISH:
45 minutes
Makes 4 servings

TIP: Buy fresh herbs in bulk to save time and money. To preserve, place the extra herbs in a blender with plenty of olive oil and purée until smooth. Pour the mixture into ice cube trays and freeze. Use the cubes in soups or stir-fry dishes. This works especially well with basil.

2 pounds eggplant, peeled and cut into cubes

2 tablespoons sea salt

¼ cup extra-virgin olive oil

1 medium yellow onion, diced

2 tablespoons chopped fresh oregano

1 tablespoon chopped fresh rosemary

3 medium tomatoes, diced

3 tablespoons red wine vinegar

3 tablespoons capers, drained

½ cup coarsely chopped pitted Kalamata olives

¾ pound bowtie (farfalle) pasta

Freshly ground black pepper, to taste

¼ cup fresh basil leaves, cut into thin strips

3 tablespoons dry-roasted pine nuts

Place the eggplant cubes in a mesh strainer over the sink. Sprinkle with salt and let stand 20 minutes. Rinse the eggplant well under cool water and pat dry with a towel.

Combine the oil and eggplant in a large, deep skillet over a medium-high flame. Sauté 4 minutes. Add the onion, oregano and rosemary and continue cooking until the onion is soft, about 6 minutes.

Add the tomatoes, vinegar, capers and olives and mix well to combine. Lower the heat to simmer and cook 15–20 minutes or until eggplant is soft.

While the sauce simmers, bring a large stockpot of lightly salted water to a boil and cook pasta until tender, about 8 minutes. Drain and set aside.

Season the sauce with pepper to taste, then remove the pan from the heat. Stir in the basil and pine nuts. Add the pasta to the skillet and toss to coat

orecchiette con cime di rapa (orecchiette pasta with savory greens)

We learned this classic Tuscan dish from a wonderful Italian cook while in Italy. It coats hearty pasta with a tangy "cheese" sauce and wilted greens.

Just about any hardy leafy green goes well in this recipe. The original uses turnip and radish greens, but we prefer kale and spinach. Collards and chard also are good.

START TO FINISH:
30 minutes
Makes 4 servings

TIP: As an alternative to soy Parmesan cheese, combine 2 slices of well-toasted bread, 1 tablespoon of nutritional yeast flakes and 1 tablespoon of vegetable broth or water in a food processor. Pulse until crumbs form. Sprinkle the mixture as you would grated Parmesan cheese.

¾ pound orecchiette pasta (for fresh, see recipe p. 109)

¼ cup extra-virgin olive oil

2 tablespoons capers, crushed with a fork

1 tablespoon red pepper flakes

½ pound bunch of kale, stalks removed, leaves cut into thin ribbons

½ cup soy Parmesan cheese

Bring a large stockpot of lightly salted water to a rolling boil and cook orecchiette until tender, about 8 minutes. Drain and set aside.

While the pasta cooks, combine the oil, capers and red pepper flakes in a large, deep skillet. Mash the capers with a fork and sauté over a medium-high flame 3–4 minutes.

Add the kale and reduce the heat to medium. Sauté 3 minutes or just until kale wilts. Add the pasta and toss.

Add the soy Parmesan cheese and toss to combine. If pasta is too dry, add several tablespoons of broth, water or additional oil.

angel hair pasta with lemon sauce

START TO FINISH:

20 minutes

Makes 4 servings

TIP: To keep fresh herbs from wilting in the refrigerator, cut away the bottom ¼ inch of stem and stand them in a glass of water. Change the water every day or so.

This fragrant and flavorful sauce complements a tangle of angel hair pasta.

2 tablespoons soy margarine

1 cup sweet white wine (Riesling works well)

2 cups vegetable broth

2 tablespoons lemon juice

1 teaspoon lemon zest

1 tablespoon minced fresh rosemary

5 fresh sage leaves, cut into thin ribbons

1 tablespoon kuzu

2 tablespoons water

½ teaspoon sea salt

¾ pound angel hair pasta

2 medium tomatoes, coarsely chopped

Melt the margarine in a medium saucepan. Add the wine and bring to a boil. Add the broth, lemon juice and zest, rosemary and sage. Simmer 3 minutes or until slightly reduced and fragrant.

In a small cup, combine the kuzu and water, stirring until a thick paste forms. Stir the paste into the sauce.

Increase the heat to medium-high and stir constantly until the sauce thickens, about 4 minutes. Remove the saucepan from the heat and stir in the salt.

Bring a large stockpot of lightly salted water to a boil and cook pasta until tender, about 8 minutes. Drain and transfer the pasta to a large serving bowl. Add the tomatoes and toss. Add the sauce and toss again to coat evenly.

olive and rosemary linguini

Here olives are the star. The recipe uses just a few ingredients to complement the rich, tangy taste of the Kalamata olives tossed with warm pasta.

START TO FINISH:

20 minutes

Makes 4 servings

- ¾ pound linguini pasta
- 2 tablespoons extra-virgin olive oil
- 1 tablespoon balsamic vinegar
- ¼ cup vegetable broth *or* dry white wine
- 2 tablespoons fresh rosemary
- 2 tablespoons fresh lavender
- 10 fresh sage leaves, coarsely chopped
- 1 medium yellow onion, diced
- 1 cup roughly chopped pitted Kalamata olives

TIP: When serving pasta with a thin or oil-based sauce, it's best to let the noodles stand 5 minutes after draining. The drier the noodles, the better the sauce will stick.

Bring a large stockpot of lightly salted water to a boil. Cook pasta until tender, about 8 minutes. Drain and set aside. Let stand 5 minutes before tossing with sauce.

While the pasta cooks, simmer the oil, vinegar and broth or wine in a large skillet over a medium flame. Add the rosemary, lavender and sage. Simmer 4–5 minutes to combine flavors and reduce the liquid.

Add the onions and olives and simmer until the onions are soft, about 6 minutes. Add the pasta and toss to combine.

apple-fried greens and orecchiette pasta

It may sound odd, but apples and pasta are a great combination. This recipe plays off the tender, juicy taste of cooked apples accented with sautéed onion. It's a great complement to the wilted kale.

START TO FINISH:

25 minutes

Makes 4 servings

TIP: To cut kale into ribbons, take 1 or 2 leaves and roll as you would a poster. Starting at the farthest end, slice the kale into thin strips.

¾ pound orecchiette pasta (For fresh, see recipe p. 109)

3 tablespoons extra-virgin olive oil

3 apples, peeled, cored and diced

1 medium onion, diced

5 fresh sage leaves, diced

½ teaspoon cinnamon

½ teaspoon sea salt

½ tablespoon curry powder

1 tablespoon sugar

1 pound kale, cut into thin ribbons

Bring a large stockpot of lightly salted water to a boil. Cook pasta until tender, about 8 minutes. Drain and set aside.

Meanwhile, in a large skillet combine the oil, apples and onion. Sauté over a medium-high flame until the apples and onions are just tender, about 5 minutes.

Add the sage, cinnamon, salt, curry powder and sugar and sauté another minute. Add the kale and cook until wilted, 2–3 minutes. Add 1–2 tablespoons of water or vegetable stock if needed for moisture.

Add the pasta to the skillet and toss to combine. Heat another 2 minutes.

poor man's pasta

The origins of this savory combination of chickpeas and pasta date back centuries in Italy. Of course fresh homemade pasta and dry beans that you soak and bake yourself taste best. But a respectable (and faster) version can be made using store-bought pasta and canned beans.

START TO FINISH:
30 minutes
Makes 4 servings

¾   **pound small, dry pasta**

2   **cloves garlic, crushed**

¼   **cup extra-virgin olive oil**

⅛   **cup white wine**

1   **tablespoon fresh rosemary leaves**

1   **tablespoon fresh thyme leaves**

¼   **cup cold water**

   15-ounce can chickpeas

½   **teaspoon freshly ground pepper**

½   **teaspoon sea salt**

TIP: Not a fan of chickpeas? Substitute just about any other canned bean, such as kidney, cranberry or fava.

Any pasta will do nicely, even spaghetti broken into pieces.

Bring a large stockpot of lightly salted water to a boil. Cook pasta until tender, about 8 minutes. Drain and set aside.

Meanwhile, in a large skillet, combine the garlic, oil and white wine and cook over a medium flame until the garlic just begins to brown. Add the rosemary and thyme and sauté an additional minute.

Add the water and chickpeas to the skillet and sauté until the beans are warm, about another 4 minutes. Add the pasta, pepper and salt, and toss to coat with oil.

spicy peanut noodles

We love peanut noodles. That's probably because we also love peanut butter and are quite happy eating it by the spoonful from the jar.

This recipe isn't quite so fattening as that, but it tastes just as good. Serve this with a simple salad and Tomato Crostini (recipe p. 6).

START TO FINISH:

20 minutes

Makes 4 servings

TIP: Don't rinse the noodles after cooking. You want them to be hot so the sauce melts and oozes into the pasta.

While the noodles cook, get all other ingredients ready to go so you can combine the noodles and sauce as quickly as possible.

1	cup Peanut Sauce (recipe p. 156)
¾	pound soba noodles
½	pound green beans, cut into 1-inch lengths
1	medium carrot, cut into matchsticks
1	cup frozen corn kernels
½	cup crushed dry-roasted peanuts
⅓	cup sesame seeds
2	tablespoons red pepper flakes

Prepare the peanut sauce and set aside.

Bring a large stockpot of water to a boil and cook noodles until al dente, about 5 minutes. Add the beans, carrots and corn to the pasta and continue cooking another 2–3 minutes or until the noodles are tender.

Drain the pasta and vegetables. Transfer to a large serving bowl. Spoon the peanut sauce over the noodles and vegetables. Sprinkle with the peanuts, sesame seeds and pepper flakes.

spicy udon noodles

Here silky noodles combine with a fiery sauce, crisp carrots and the tangy arame sea vegetable for a great convergence of taste and texture.

START TO FINISH:

45 minutes

(15 minutes active)

Makes 2–4 servings

TIP: We prefer to use natural hot sauces rather than those commonly found in Asian markets. Those can contain chemicals and preservatives that give the dish a metallic, simulated taste. The real thing should contain little more than hot peppers, vinegar and natural seasonings.

- ½ ounce (dry weight) arame seaweed
- 3 tablespoons toasted sesame seed oil
- 3 cloves garlic, cut into quarters
- ¼ cup umeboshi plum vinegar
- ¼ cup roasted tahini
- 1 cup water
- 1 teaspoon hot pepper sauce
- 8 ounces udon noodles
- 2 carrots, ends trimmed, cut into matchsticks
- ¼ cup slivered almonds, for garnish (optional)

Place the arame in a medium bowl and cover with water. Soak until pliable, about 30 minutes. Once soft, drain and rinse the arame in a mesh strainer.

Heat 1 tablespoon of the sesame oil in a medium skillet over a medium flame. Add the arame and sauté 5 minutes. Keep warm.

In a small skillet over a medium flame, sauté the garlic in the remaining sesame oil. When the garlic begins to brown, transfer it and the oil to a blender or food processor. Add the vinegar, tahini, 1 cup water and hot pepper sauce and purée until smooth. Return the mixture to the skillet and heat over a very low flame 2–3 minutes. Keep warm.

Bring a large stockpot of water to a boil. Add the noodles and cook until tender, about 8 minutes. Drain.

Toss the noodles, arame and carrots in a large serving bowl. Top the pasta with the almonds and drizzle with the garlic sauce.

pad thai

No need to eat out to get great Pad Thai. We like it hot and crunchy.

¾ pound dry wide rice noodles

⅓ cup lime juice

2 tablespoons soy sauce

2 tablespoons brown rice syrup or sugar

½ teaspoon hot pepper sauce

⅔ cup hot water

1 tablespoon tamarind concentrate

1½ tablespoons peanut oil

1 medium carrot

2 tablespoons toasted sesame seed oil

2 teaspoons minced fresh ginger

3 cloves garlic, minced (about 1 tablespoon)

5 scallions (green and white parts), finely diced

1 cup mung bean sprouts

½ cup crushed dry-roasted peanuts

1 tablespoon red pepper flakes

START TO FINISH:

30 minutes

Makes 4 servings

TIP: Many so-called Pad Thai noodles actually contain egg, so read labels carefully. We find that many other Asian pastas, such as udon or soba noodles, work well.

Bring a medium stockpot of water to a boil. Remove the pot from the heat and add the rice noodles. Soak about 20 minutes, until tender. Drain and set aside.

Meanwhile, whisk together the lime juice, soy sauce, brown rice syrup, hot pepper sauce, water, tamarind concentrate and peanut oil in a small bowl, mixing 1–2 minutes to dissolve.

Shave the carrot into thin strips using a vegetable peeler. Heat the sesame oil in a wok or large, deep sauté pan over a medium-high flame. Add the ginger and garlic and sauté 30 seconds. Add the carrots and scallions and sauté 2 minutes.

Reduce heat to low, add the lime juice mixture and simmer 1 minute. Add the noodles and toss to coat. Sauté about 2 minutes. Remove from heat, then add the sprouts and toss to combine.

Garnish with peanuts and red pepper flakes.

sweet-and-sour tempeh with udon

START TO FINISH:

45 minutes

Makes 4 servings

TIP: Serve over a generous helping of steamed greens.

The sweet-and-sour sauce in this dish is nothing like the fluorescent goo most Asian restaurants serve. It is delicately sweet, with just a hint of sour.

- 1 cup apple juice
- 1 cup pineapple juice
- 1 cup vegetable broth
-   8-ounce package of tempeh, cut into 12–14 squares
- 1 medium onion, diced
- 2 large carrots, ends trimmed, cut into thin rounds
- ½ cup baby corn
- 1 stalk celery, diced
- 1 cup chopped broccoli florets
- 2 teaspoons brown rice vinegar
- 2 tablespoons maple syrup
- 2 tablespoons cranberry juice
- ½ teaspoon lemon juice
- 1 teaspoon soy sauce
- 8 ounces udon noodles
- 2 tablespoons kuzu or arrowroot powder
- ¼ cup cool water
- ½ cup dry-roasted cashews (optional)
- ¼ cup chopped scallions, for garnish

Combine the apple and pineapple juices and vegetable broth in a medium saucepan over a high flame. Add the tempeh and bring to a boil. Reduce heat to low and simmer 15 minutes.

Bring a medium stockpot of lightly salted water to a boil.

Add the onion, carrots, corn and celery to the tempeh and cook an additional 5 minutes. Add broccoli and cook another 2 minutes.

Add the vinegar, maple syrup, cranberry juice, lemon juice and soy sauce and stir to combine. Simmer 1 minute.

Using a slotted spoon, transfer the vegetables and tempeh to a bowl, leaving the cooking liquid in the saucepan. Cover the vegetables and tempeh to keep warm.

Add the noodles to the boiling water and cook until tender, about 6 minutes. Drain and set aside.

Meanwhile, return the saucepan of cooking liquid to the stove over a low flame.

In a small glass, mix the kuzu or arrowroot in ¼ cup water, then add to the pan. Add the cashews, if desired. Stir sauce constantly over a low flame until the mixture thickens, 3–4 minutes.

Arrange vegetables and tempeh over a bed of noodles. Ladle sweet-and-sour sauce over the top and garnish with scallions.

grains
and legumes

Yummy

3x dressing
3x tomatos
diced peppers + cukes

chickpea and bulgur pilaf

Serve this as a side dish or stuff into a pita pocket for a great tasting lunch.

- 1 cup uncooked bulgur or cracked wheat
- 1 cup boiling water
- 1 cup diced tomato (seeds and juice discarded)
- 1 cup chopped scallions
- ½ cup chopped fresh flat-leaf parsley
- 1 teaspoon chopped fresh basil
- 16-ounce can chickpeas, drained and rinsed
- 1½ teaspoons grated lemon zest
- ¼ cup lemon juice
- 3 tablespoons extra-virgin olive oil
- ½ teaspoon sea salt
- Freshly ground black pepper, to taste

Place the bulgur in a large bowl. Add boiling water and stir to mix. Cover the bowl with plastic wrap and let stand 30 minutes.

Combine the tomato, scallions, parsley, basil and chickpeas in a medium bowl. Toss well, then add to bulgur and stir to mix.

In a separate bowl, whisk together the zest, juice, oil, salt and pepper. Add mixture to bulgur and toss well. Let stand 10 minutes before serving.

START TO FINISH.
40 minutes
Makes 2 servings *(makes 4)*

TIP: Substitute any leftover whole grain for the bulgur.

Tzatziki (recipe p. 156), is the perfect topping for this dish.

steamed vegetables with curry couscous

Couscous is great for its speed and light nutty flavor. While rice can take close to an hour, couscous is ready in just 5 minutes.

START TO FINISH:

45 minutes

Makes 4 servings

TIP: Couscous typically is available in regular and whole wheat. In terms of taste, the difference is negligible. Opt for whole wheat, which packs more nutrients.

1 medium yellow onion, coarsely chopped

1 red bell pepper, seeded and coarsely chopped

1 medium carrot, cut into thin rounds

2 small sweet potatoes, cubed

½ small cauliflower, cut into small florets (about 3 cups)

4 tomatoes, coarsely chopped (juice retained)

   15-ounce can kidney beans

1 cup golden raisins

½ cup dried cranberries (unsweetened are best)

½ teaspoon sea salt

½ teaspoon ground cumin

½ teaspoon garam masala

1¼ cups water

1 tablespoon extra-virgin olive oil

1 teaspoon curry powder

¼ teaspoon chili powder

1 cup uncooked couscous

Bring 1 inch of water to a boil in a medium saucepan fitted with a steamer basket. Add the onion, pepper, carrot, sweet potatoes and cauliflower and cover.

Steam the vegetables 5 minutes or until cauliflower is just tender. Uncover and set aside.

In a large saucepan, combine the tomatoes, beans, raisins, cranberries, salt, cumin and garam masala. Simmer over a medium flame 12 minutes or until the raisins and cranberries are tender.

Add the steamed vegetables to the tomato mixture and stir to coat. Reduce the heat to low, cover and simmer 10 minutes.

Meanwhile, bring 1¼ cups of water to a boil in a small saucepan. Add the oil, curry powder and chili powder. Cover and boil another minute. Add the couscous, cover and remove from heat. Let stand 5 minutes. Uncover the couscous and fluff with a fork.

To serve, arrange about ⅔ cup of couscous on each plate, then spoon heaping portions of vegetables on top.

couscous curry with dried fruit

Here's a way to pack plenty of flavor into a simple grain dish.

START TO FINISH:

25 minutes

Makes 4 servings

TIP: Don't have corn? Use peas or diced carrots. Use them even if you do have corn. The same goes for the dried fruit. To make this more of an autumn dish, use dried apples instead of mango.

If you make this dish the night before, reserve the dressing to toss with the couscous just before serving.

SALAD

- 1½ cups water
- 1 teaspoon extra-virgin olive oil
- 1½ cups uncooked couscous
- ½ cup dried cranberries
- ½ cup dried cherries
- ½ cup dried mango, cut into small cubes
- 1 cup frozen corn kernels
- 1 teaspoon curry powder
- ¼ cup sliced scallions
- ¼ cup chopped fresh dill
- 15-ounce can chickpeas

DRESSING

- ½ cup orange juice
- ½ cup unsweetened cranberry juice
- 3 tablespoons toasted sesame seed oil
- ½ teaspoon sea salt
- ¼ teaspoon freshly ground black pepper
- 1 tablespoon lemon juice

Bring the water and olive oil to a boil in medium saucepan. Add the couscous, cover and remove the pan from the heat. Let stand 5 minutes.

Remove the lid and fluff the couscous with a fork. Add remaining salad ingredients and mix to combine. Cover the pan and set aside 10 minutes or until corn has thawed.

For the dressing, whisk together all ingredients in a small bowl.

To serve, toss the couscous mixture with the dressing in a medium bowl. Serve at room temperature. If chilled overnight, let stand at room temperature 1 hour before serving.

honey mustard tempeh over couscous

When you're hankering for something meaty (even vegetarians sometimes want that heavy, stick-to-your-ribs sort of meal), try this sweet and tangy tempeh dish

Like tofu, tempeh complements and absorbs the flavors of whatever it is cooked with, giving even the most delicate marinades a bold presence on the plate.

START TO FINISH:
30 minutes
Makes 2 servings

TIP: When recipes call for heavy skillets, try cast iron. These inexpensive pans are extremely durable and cook evenly. They also hold heat longer.

2 tablespoons sesame seed oil

2 carrots, ends trimmed, cut to matchsticks

1 medium yellow onion, diced

8-ounce package of tempeh, cut into 6 pieces

1 ½ cups apple juice

2 tablespoons honey

3 tablespoons Dijon mustard

1 tablespoon yellow mustard powder

1 ½ cups water

2 tablespoons extra-virgin olive oil

1 cup uncooked couscous

2 tablespoons kuzu

Heat the sesame oil in a heavy skillet over a medium-high flame. Sauté the carrots and onion until tender, about 5 minutes. Add the tempeh and brown lightly on both sides, about 3 minutes per side.

In a small bowl, whisk together the apple juice, honey, Dijon mustard and mustard powder. Add the juice mixture to the tempeh and simmer another 5 minutes.

While the tempeh simmers, bring 1 cup of water to a boil in a small saucepan. Add olive oil and couscous. Cover the pan and remove from heat. Let stand 5 minutes, then uncover and fluff with a fork.

Combine the kuzu and ½ cup water in a glass and mix thoroughly to dissolve. Add the kuzu mixture to the tempeh and stir the sauce until it thickens, about 3 minutes.

Serve tempeh pieces over a bed of couscous with sauce drizzled over the top.

vegetarian haggis

Few dishes are less vegetarian friendly than haggis, a Scottish dish of diced sheep innards cooked with seasonings and grains inside a sheep's stomach. This version does away with the sheep parts.

START TO FINISH:

1 hour

Makes 8 servings

TIP: Even if this isn't a traditional version of haggis, you still can serve it the traditional way—accompanied by mashed potatoes. A drizzle of gravy is nice, too. For an Americanization, try it with ketchup.

The haggis can be baked in a loaf pan, but it is easier and more attractive to cook individual portions in ramekins or muffin tins.

1	small yellow onion, finely diced
1	tablespoon extra-virgin olive oil
2	tablespoons natural shortening
1	medium carrot, finely grated
1	cup button mushrooms, diced
¾	cup red lentils
2	cups vegetable stock
1	cup canned kidney beans, mashed
¾	cup mixed nuts, finely ground
2	tablespoons soy sauce
1	tablespoon lemon juice
1	teaspoon finely chopped fresh rosemary
	Pinch cayenne pepper
	Sea salt and freshly ground black pepper, to taste
3	cups quick-cooking oatmeal
½	cup Scotch
½	cup water

Preheat the oven to 375°F.

Combine the onion, oil and shortening in a large skillet over a medium-high flame. Sauté until onions are just tender, about 4 minutes. Add the carrots and mushrooms and sauté another 3 minutes.

Add the lentils and 1½ cups stock and bring to a simmer.

Combine the kidney beans with the remaining ½ cup stock. Add the beans, nuts, soy sauce, lemon juice, rosemary, cayenne, salt and pepper to the lentils. Cover, reduce heat to low and simmer 10 minutes.

Stir in the oatmeal, Scotch and water and remove from the flame.

Lightly oil 8 ramekins. Spoon the mixture into ramekins, cover with foil and bake 30 minutes. Uncover during the final 5 minutes. Let cool 10 minutes before serving.

START TO FINISH:

30 minutes

Makes 4 servings

TIP: Don't skimp on spices. Buy the best, and buy in small quantities. Don't use spices that have sat in the cupboard for years. Most spices, while safe to use, lose their potency after a year. Buy little and buy often.

three-bean curry

Homemade curry—that potent blend of aromatic spices—is so much better than anything from a jar. The list of ingredients may seem daunting, but this dish is easy to throw together and can be on the table in 30 minutes.

Serve this over a bed of steamed basmati rice or couscous.

- 2 medium potatoes, diced
-   15-ounce can kidney beans
-   15-ounce can navy or Great Northern beans
-   15-ounce can chickpeas
- 4 tablespoons extra-virgin olive oil
- 2 medium onions, diced
- 1 teaspoon ground cloves
- 1 teaspoon freshly ground black pepper
- 2 bay leaves
- 1 teaspoon cinnamon
- 4 garlic cloves
-   1-inch piece fresh ginger
- 5 tablespoons water
- 1 teaspoon coriander seeds
- 1 teaspoon ground cumin
- ½ teaspoon garam masala
- 1 teaspoon chili powder
- ½ teaspoon turmeric
-   Pinch mace
-   Pinch nutmeg
- ½ teaspoon sea salt
-   15-ounce can diced tomatoes or 3 medium tomatoes, diced
- 1 medium carrot, cut into matchsticks

Bring 2 inches of water to a boil in a large saucepan fitted with a steamer basket. Add the potatoes to the basket, cover and steam 8 minutes or until just tender when pierced with a fork.

Meanwhile, place the kidney beans, navy beans and chickpeas in a mesh strainer and rinse under cool water. Drain well.

In a large, heavy-bottomed skillet, combine the oil, half of the diced onion, cloves, pepper, bay leaves and cinnamon. Sauté over a medium flame 3–4 minutes or until the onions are tender.

Combine the garlic, ginger, water and remaining onion in a blender or food processor and process until smooth. Add the mixture to the skillet and sauté another 4 minutes.

Stir in the coriander, cumin, garam masala, chili, turmeric, mace, nutmeg and salt. Simmer 5 minutes. Remove and discard bay leaves.

Stir in the beans and tomatoes. Simmer 5 minutes, then add potatoes. Simmer another 3 minutes. Serve immediately garnished with carrot sticks.

bean croquettes with zesty marinara

The beans in these croquettes go well with a fiery marinara. A sweet and spicy salsa also makes a nice sauce.

CROQUETTES:

	15-ounce can navy beans
2	tablespoons vegetable broth
1	tablespoon lime juice
½	cup breadcrumbs
½	cup finely grated carrot
⅓	cup corn kernels
1	tablespoon red pepper flakes
1	teaspoon paprika
1	teaspoon ground cumin
¼	teaspoon chili powder
	Sea salt and freshly ground black pepper, to taste
2	tablespoons extra-virgin olive oil

SAUCE:

3	tomatoes, chopped (seeds and juices retained)
½	cup vegetable broth
1	tablespoon grated fresh ginger
1	teaspoon hot pepper sauce
2	tablespoons minced fresh cilantro
1	teaspoon dried thyme

START TO FINISH:

45 minutes

Makes 4 servings

TIP: To make breadcrumbs, toast several slices of whole wheat bread at a low heat several times or until they are dry and hard but not burned. Crumble the bread into a food processor and pulse until crumbs are formed. Add seasonings (such as garlic powder) and a drizzle of olive oil to give the crumbs more flavor.

Preheat the oven to 400°F. Lightly oil a baking sheet.

Pulse the beans for several seconds in a food processor or until coarsely chopped. Add remaining croquette ingredients except the oil and pulse for several seconds or until ingredients are just combined.

Transfer the mixture to a bowl. Use your hands to form four ½-inch-thick patties. Place the patties on the prepared baking sheet. Drizzle the tops of the patties with oil.

Bake the patties 15 minutes or until the tops begin to brown. Use a spatula to flip the patties and bake an additional 15–20 minutes or until lightly browned.

While the patties bake, combine all sauce ingredients in a small saucepan. Cover and bring to a simmer over a medium flame. Cook 8 minutes, stirring frequently.

To serve, ladle several tablespoons of sauce over each croquette.

peppery pumpkin risotto

We love the sinful taste of risotto, all thick and creamy. The pumpkin gives this dish a beautiful color and a rich flavor.

1¾	cups **Arborio rice**
2	tablespoons **extra-virgin olive oil**
1	tablespoon **soy margarine**
1	small **yellow onion, diced**
½	cup **sweet white wine, such as Riesling**
4½	cups **vegetable broth**
1½	cups **cooked pumpkin or 15-ounce can pumpkin purée**
1½	teaspoons **grated fresh ginger**
¼	teaspoon **cayenne pepper**
¾	teaspoon **sea salt**
¼	teaspoon **freshly ground black pepper**
¼	cup **soy Parmesan cheese**

Rinse the rice in a mesh strainer and drain.

In a large skillet, combine the oil, margarine and onion and sauté over a medium flame until the onions are soft, about 6 minutes.

Add the rice and stir well until coated with the oil and margarine. Increase the heat to medium-high and add the wine. Stir constantly until the wine has been absorbed.

Begin to add broth, ½ cup at a time, stirring constantly and adding more liquid as it is absorbed.

When the rice has absorbed the broth, reduce the flame to medium-low. Taste to check the texture. The rice should be firm but cooked through. If the rice is too hard or dry, add additional broth, ½ cup at a time. When the rice is at the desired texture, stir in the pumpkin, ginger and cayenne pepper.

Cook 2–3 minutes, then add salt, black pepper and soy Parmesan and mix well. Serve immediately.

shortcut artichoke risotto

This speedy take on the classic Italian dish puts creamy risotto on your plate in just minutes and is great for using leftover rice.

3 tablespoons extra-virgin olive oil

1 medium yellow onion, diced

2 tablespoons chopped fresh dill

2 tablespoons chopped fresh parsley

2 cups cooked white or brown rice

¾ cup vegetable broth

Sea salt and freshly ground black pepper, to taste

1 tablespoon nutritional yeast flakes

8 artichoke hearts (8 ½–ounce can), thinly sliced

3 tablespoons soy Parmesan cheese

In a large skillet, combine the oil and onion and sauté over a medium flame until the onions are translucent, about 6 minutes. Stir in the dill and parsley, and cook another 2 minutes.

Stir in the rice and broth. The mixture should be sticky and wet but not runny. If the rice is too dry, add another ¼ cup of broth.

Season with salt and pepper to taste, then stir in the yeast flakes and artichokes. Heat another 4 minutes, stirring frequently, until the artichokes and rice are hot.

Stir in the soy Parmesan just before serving.

START TO FINISH:
25 minutes
Makes 2 servings

TIP: If you don't have leftovers, make plain rice as you normally would. You don't save time, but this risotto still is easier than traditional recipes.

Brown rice is fine for this version, but use white Arborio rice when making traditional risotto. Arborio is especially starchy—key to the dish's creaminess.

pesto rice with seitan

Fresh pesto lends a richness to this dish, while chunks of seitan and tomato give it a meaty consistency and appealing color.

START TO FINISH:

15 minutes

Makes 4 servings

TIP: The pesto calls for nutritional yeast flakes, which are available at most natural food stores. For a substitute, try an equal amount of soy Parmesan cheese.

2 tablespoons soy sauce

2 tablespoons vegetable broth or water

¼ pound seitan, cut in ½-inch cubes

½ teaspoon freshly ground black pepper

3 cups cooked short-grain brown rice

½ cup pesto (recipe p. 158)

12 cherry tomatoes

2 tablespoons chopped fresh chives

Heat the soy sauce and 2 tablespoons of the vegetable broth or water in a large skillet over a medium flame. Add the seitan and stir to coat with sauce. Add the pepper and cook until the seitan is browned and the sauce begins to reduce, about 5 minutes.

Add the rice to the skillet and toss to combine. Cook until the rice absorbs any remaining sauce, about 3–4 minutes.

Spoon about ¾ cup of the rice and seitan mixture onto each dish. Top each serving with 2–3 tablespoons of pesto. Garnish with several cherry tomatoes and sprinkle with chives.

citrus cilantro rice

This tangy rice is great served warm with roasted vegetables or chilled and tossed with salad greens and cherry tomatoes.

To add more pizzazz, garnish with tangerine segments just before serving.

START TO FINISH:
1 hour
Makes 2 servings

- 2 teaspoons extra-virgin olive oil
- 1 cup long-grain brown rice
- 2 cups vegetable broth
- ½ teaspoon orange zest
- ½ teaspoon lemon zest
- ½ teaspoon lime zest
- 1 cup frozen peas
- 1 tablespoon chopped fresh cilantro
- 4 scallions, diced (about ⅓ cup)
- ¼ cup almond slivers
- 2 tablespoons seasoned brown rice vinegar

TIP: To avoid spending a fortune on olive oil, buy two types: a pricey one for drizzling raw over salads, crostini and other uncooked foods and a cheaper one for baking and sautéing. Heating dulls the taste of even the most expensive oils.

Combine the oil and rice in a medium skillet and sauté over a medium-high flame 3 minutes or until the rice just begins to brown.

Add the broth, zests, peas and cilantro. Bring to a boil. Reduce heat to low and cover. Simmer 40 minutes or until rice is tender and liquid has been absorbed.

Uncover and cool 10 minutes. Transfer rice to a serving bowl and toss with scallions, almond slivers and vinegar.

spanish-style brown rice

Rice and peas are staples in most of the Spanish-speaking Caribbean. Pump additional taste and nutrition into this dish by using brown rice instead of the traditional white and adding more vegetables.

START TO FINISH:

1 hour

Makes 4 servings

TIP: Saffron is pricey. For an inexpensive substitute, use ⅛ teaspoon turmeric. The flavor will be different, but the dish still will be colorful and delicious.

2 tablespoons extra-virgin olive oil

2 medium leeks, white and light green parts only, sliced thin

2 medium carrots, ends trimmed, diced

1 medium red bell pepper, seeded and diced

3 cloves garlic, minced

5–6 saffron threads

½ teaspoon lemon zest

3 cups vegetable broth

Pinch of sea salt

2 cups long-grain brown rice

10-ounce package frozen peas

2 tablespoons lemon juice

2 tablespoons chopped fresh parsley leaves

Combine the oil, leeks, carrots and red peppers in a large skillet and heat over a medium-high flame. Sauté 5 minutes. Stir in the garlic, saffron and zest and cook 1 minute.

Add the broth and salt and bring to a boil. Add the rice and return to a boil. Cover and simmer 40 minutes.

Stir in the peas and juice. Cover pan and cook an additional 5 minutes.

Remove the pan from heat and let stand 5 minutes, covered. Remove the cover and sprinkle with parsley. Fluff the rice with a fork.

tomato and coconut milk rice

Hot peppers add fire to this dish from Mozambique, but they are mellowed by sweet coconut milk.

2	tablespoons peanut oil
½	medium yellow onion, finely chopped
1	small hot pepper, such as habenero, seeded and chopped
1	cup Arborio rice
1½	cups coconut milk
2	medium tomatoes, chopped
1	teaspoon sea salt
1½	teaspoons crushed red pepper

In a large skillet, heat the oil over a medium flame and sauté the onion and pepper until they are soft, about 5 minutes.

Add the rice and cook, stirring constantly, until the grains are evenly coated with oil, about 3 minutes. Add the coconut milk, tomatoes and salt and bring to a simmer over a medium flame.

Cover the pan, reduce the heat to low and simmer until all the liquid is absorbed and the rice is tender, about 20 minutes. Add more water or coconut milk if the rice is not quite tender.

Remove the skillet from the heat and stir in the crushed pepper. Cover and let stand 10 minutes before serving.

START TO FINISH:

45 minutes

Makes 4 servings

TIP: Always wear rubber gloves while working with hot peppers; the oils can irritate skin.

umbrian baked beans

The traditional version of this Italian dish calls for soaking dry beans overnight, then cooking them several hours. We've updated the recipe using convenient canned beans. Serve this alongside steamed vegetables and fresh bread, or in a pita pocket.

¼	cup extra-virgin olive oil
2	tablespoons fresh basil leaves
1	tablespoon chopped fresh rosemary leaves
3	tablespoons capers, drained
½	tablespoon Dijon mustard
1	teaspoon sea salt
Two	15-ounce cans navy beans

Preheat the oven to 350°F. Combine the oil, basil, rosemary, capers, mustard and salt in a food processor or blender and process until smooth.

In a small baking dish, mix the beans with the sauce. Cover with foil and bake 30 minutes.

START TO FINISH:
35 minutes
Makes 3 servings

TIP: In warmer months, serve this room temperature over a bed of mixed greens and chilled noodles sprinkled with balsamic vinegar and olive oil.

Try mixing up the beans, perhaps a combination of navy, fava and chickpea.

belizean beans and rice

In Belizean cuisine, coconut milk is ubiquitous, showing up in everything from stewed beef to boiled bananas. In this simple rice and beans dish, a staple in Belize, the coconut transforms simple ingredients with sweet, lush overtones.

START TO FINISH:

45 minutes

Makes 4 servings

TIP: Flame tamers—flat metal disks placed beneath pots to evenly disperse heat—are essential to prevent burning when cooking rice and other dishes that simmer low and long. Flame tamers are inexpensive and available at most kitchen supply shops.

2 cups (1½ 15-ounce cans) pinto beans, with liquid

1 small green bell pepper, seeded and diced

1 small yellow onion, diced

2 tablespoons fresh cilantro, chopped

4 tablespoons soy margarine

   15-ounce can coconut milk

2 cups long-grain white rice, rinsed

   Sea salt and freshly ground black pepper, to taste

⅛ teaspoon chili powder

⅛ teaspoon celery seed

⅛ teaspoon ground coriander

⅛ teaspoon nutmeg

⅛ teaspoon onion powder

⅛ teaspoon paprika

⅛ garlic powder

Combine all ingredients in a large saucepan and bring to a boil over a medium flame. Cover and simmer 30 minutes. Fluff rice with a fork just before serving.

cuban black beans and rice

Here's a simplified version of a Cuban favorite.

- 3 tablespoons extra-virgin olive oil
- ½ cup chopped soy sausage, uncooked
- 1 cup chopped yellow onion
- 3 cloves garlic, minced
- ½ green bell pepper, seeded and diced
- 2 cups short-grain brown rice
- ½ cup tomato sauce
- 4 cups vegetable broth
- 1 teaspoon ground cumin
- 1 teaspoon oregano
- ½ teaspoon freshly ground black pepper
- Two 15-ounce cans black beans, drained and rinsed
- 1 bay leaf

In a large stockpot, combine the oil and sausage and sauté 3 minutes over a medium flame. Add the onion, garlic and pepper and sauté 2 minutes. Add rice and sauté another 2 minutes.

Stir in the tomato sauce and broth. Bring to a boil. Add the remaining ingredients and return to a boil. Cover, reduce heat to low and simmer 40 minutes, stirring occasionally. Discard bay leaf before serving.

START TO FINISH:
50 minutes
Makes 4 servings

TIP: Don't do garlic? Or don't like what it does to you? Try using 2 tablespoons of diced scallions for each clove of garlic called for.

nut loaf

This recipe was inspired by a nut loaf we sampled during a visit to England. A farmer's wife made this for us and was kind enough to share her recipe.

It took quite a while, but we finally made a version that didn't rely on butter and eggs. And it is great with gravy.

START TO FINISH:

1 hour, 15 minutes
Makes 8 servings

TIP: When chopping nuts and seeds, be careful to use only the pulse setting. It is easy to go from chopped peanuts to peanut butter in just seconds.

1 cup peanuts, raw and unsalted

1 cup sunflower seeds, raw and unsalted

½ cup almonds, raw and unsalted

½ cup cashew nuts, raw and unsalted

1 medium carrot, finely grated

1 medium onion, finely grated

1 medium apple, finely grated

1 tablespoon extra-virgin olive oil

  6-ounce can tomato paste

3 tablespoons peanut butter

1 tablespoon soy sauce

1 tablespoon balsamic vinegar

1 tablespoon vegetarian Worcestershire sauce (traditional Worcestershire sauces contain anchovies)

Preheat the oven to 350°F.

Place the nuts and seeds on a baking sheet and dry roast in the oven 12–15 minutes or until lightly golden. Remove from the oven and cool, about 10 minutes. Leave the oven on.

Transfer the nuts and seeds to a food processor and pulse until a coarse meal is formed. Transfer the mixture to a bowl and add remaining ingredients. Mix until well combined. The mixture should be thick and sticky.

Lightly oil a loaf pan. Transfer the mixture to the prepared pan and smooth the top. Bake 30 minutes. If the top browns too soon, cover with foil for the remaining baking time.

Remove the loaf from the oven and let stand 15 minutes.

To serve, run a sharp knife along the edges of the loaf to separate it from the pan. Place a large plate upside down over the loaf and invert it to remove the loaf from the pan. Slice and serve.

sauces, dressings and marinades

silky raspberry vinaigrette

This versatile vinaigrette has just the right combination of tangy bite and sweet fruit to bring out the best in summer salads. During colder months, warm it and pour over steamed vegetables.

The secret is high-quality peppercorns (available at natural food and gourmet stores), a light, fruity olive oil and the very best all-fruit raspberry jam.

START TO FINISH: 5 MINUTES

Makes ½ cup

TIP: Any type of vinegar will do. For light salads with lots of bright, crisp vegetables such as red peppers, carrots and onions, try a cider or brown rice vinegar. For heartier salads that might include cubes of roasted tofu and tempeh or crunchy croutons, try a bold balsamic vinegar.

  6 tablespoons extra-virgin olive oil

1½ tablespoons balsamic vinegar

  ½ teaspoon freshly ground black pepper

  2 tablespoons all-fruit raspberry jam

  ½ teaspoon sea salt

Combine all ingredients in a blender and purée until smooth. Alternatively, place the ingredients in a jar with a tight-fitting lid and shake vigorously.

Store the dressing in the refrigerator in a tightly covered jar. Bring the dressing to room temperature and shake well before serving.

peach salsa

Try this sweet and spicy salsa with nacho chips, drizzled over a tortilla wrapped around beans and sautéed onions or tossed with pasta.

START TO FINISH: 20 MINUTES

Makes about 2 cups

TIP: This recipe calls for hot peppers but doesn't specify the variety or quantity. Add peppers according to taste, keeping in mind that the seeds add heat. Remove any seeds if you prefer a mild salsa. We use 2 habeneros with most seeds removed for a mild salsa. The salsa will keep about 1 week refrigerated.

  1 pound very ripe tomatoes, cored and cut into quarters

  2 peaches, pitted and cut into quarters

  ½ large yellow onion, coarsely diced

     Juice of 1 lemon

  1 tablespoon fresh cilantro, diced (leaves only)

  3 tablespoons fresh parsley, diced (leaves only)

  1 teaspoon fresh dill, diced

     Hot peppers, diced, to taste

  3 tablespoons extra-virgin olive oil

  3 tablespoons cider vinegar

  1 tablespoon sea salt

Combine all ingredients in a food processor. Pulse in 1-second intervals for about 20 pulses to blend all ingredients. Transfer the salsa to a bowl and refrigerate 1 hour.

sweet nut sauce

Great warm or room temperature, this sauce is delicious over grains or steamed vegetables. It is a favorite of the Kushi Institute, a great source of information on the connection between diet and health.

START TO FINISH: 5 MINUTES

Makes 3 cups

TIP: Brown rice vinegar generally comes in two varieties—seasoned and unseasoned. Seasoned vinegar has a wonderful taste, but be careful when buying. If you buy brands that are not organic, they likely have added chemicals and sugars.

- 1 cup apple juice
- 1 cup cashew nut butter
- 1 cup brown rice vinegar
- ⅓ cup soy sauce

Combine all ingredients in a blender or food processor and process until smooth. Serve room temperature or heat over a low flame until warm.

Store the sauce in a tightly covered glass jar in the refrigerator for up to 1 week.

miso marinade

This easy-to-make marinade goes well on just about anything, from vegetables to tofu, tempeh to seitan. Baste ears of corn with it and cook them on the grill

START TO FINISH: 5 MINUTES

Makes 1 cup

TIP: There are many ways to grill corn on the cob. Our favorite is to husk the corn, then soak the ears in a bowl of water 15–20 minutes. Place them, still dripping wet, on the hot grill and baste with marinade. Turn the ears frequently and baste repeatedly until done, about 5 minutes.

- 4 tablespoons dark miso (barley is good)
- 3 tablespoons mirin
- 3 tablespoons red wine
- 2 tablespoons brown rice vinegar
- 2 teaspoons toasted sesame seed oil
- 2 cloves garlic
- 1 teaspoon nori flakes
- 1-inch piece of fresh ginger
- ½ teaspoon red pepper flakes

Combine all ingredients in a blender or food processor and purée until smooth.

peanut sauce

This is one of our favorites, and we will eat it with anything. Try it as the dipping sauce for Fresh Spring Rolls (recipe p. 14), or toss it with warm noodles.

Using a hot pepper sauce instead of just paprika and hot pepper flakes (as most recipes call for) gives the sauce uniform heat. And the maple syrup and brown rice vinegar complement the spices without overpowering.

This sauce will store in the refrigerator up to a week. It can be made just before serving or is even better if it has a few hours for the flavors to combine.

START TO FINISH: 5 MINUTES
Makes about 1½ cups

TIP: To reduce the fat in this recipe, substitute 3 tablespoons of soft, silken tofu for an equal amount of the peanut butter.

- ¼ cup soy sauce
- ⅛ cup brown rice vinegar
- ⅓ cup water
- 1 tablespoon maple syrup
- ½ teaspoon sea salt
- 1-inch piece fresh ginger
- ⅔ cup chunky peanut butter (more or less depending on desired thickness)
- 2 tablespoons toasted sesame seed oil
- ½ teaspoon paprika
- 1–2 teaspoons hot pepper sauce

Combine all ingredients in a blender or food processor and purée until smooth. Adjust peanut butter and water for desired consistency. Serve immediately or chill. If chilled, let come to room temperature before serving.

tzatziki

Tzatziki is a cool and flavorful Greek yogurt dip made with cucumber and dill. It is a perfect topping for spicy foods. It also is good spread on warm flatbread. This version uses soy yogurt.

START TO FINISH: 5 MINUTES
Makes 1 cup

TIP: To make this recipe especially thick and creamy, drain any water from the top of the yogurt before preparing.

- 1 medium English cucumber, peeled and seeded
- 1 teaspoon sea salt
- 1 cup plain soy yogurt
- 2 tablespoons lemon juice
- 2 tablespoons minced fresh dill
- 1 clove garlic, minced

Dice the cucumber and place in a small bowl. Mix in remaining ingredients and refrigerate 30 minutes to let flavors combine.

peppery apricot sauce

Though we think it's almost a sin to eat fresh spring rolls with anything but Peanut Sauce (recipe p. 156), for those with a sweet tooth, this is a good alternative. Or try it drizzled over Pad Thai (recipe p. 127).

START TO FINISH: 5 MINUTES
Makes 1 cup

TIP: To substitute fresh apricots for the jam, pit them and slice into chunks. Use about 1 cup and 1 tablespoon maple syrup or brown rice syrup. For dried apricots, soak ½ cup apricots in warm water 25 minutes, then cut into chunks. Use the same amount of sweetener as for fresh.

- 3 tablespoons brown rice vinegar
- 1-inch piece fresh ginger
- 1 clove garlic
- 2 tablespoons lemon juice
- ½ cup all-fruit apricot jam
- ¼ teaspoon sea salt
- ¼ teaspoon hot pepper sauce
- ¼ cup chopped scallion, for garnish

Combine all ingredients except the scallions in a food processor or blender and purée until smooth.

Serve at room temperature or warmed slightly, garnished with scallions. To warm, transfer to a small saucepan and heat over a low flame 3–4 minutes.

succulent strawberry and vinegar sauce

This sweet, tangy sauce is a treat from Umbria, a province of central Italy.

The sauce is simple to make, but it carries complex flavors. Try it drizzled over steamed vegetables, such as cauliflower and broccoli, or tossed with fresh pasta. For a real treat, spoon a little over vanilla nondairy "ice cream."

If vinegar and "ice cream" sound like a strange mix, that thought will vanish as soon as you taste it.

START TO FINISH: 15 MINUTES
Makes 1 cup

TIP: Raspberry or other berry jams also are good in this recipe. But be sure to stick with jams with bold flavors. Mellower ones, such as apricot, can't compete with the flavor of the vinegar and the sauce loses its balance.

- 1 cup balsamic vinegar
- 3 tablespoons all-fruit strawberry jam
- 2 tablespoons brown rice or maple syrup

Combine all ingredients in a small, heavy saucepan. Heat over a medium flame and bring to a foaming simmer. Reduce heat to low and simmer 8–10 minutes or until thick. Refrigerate in a tightly covered glass jar up to 2 weeks.

umeboshi pumpkin seed dressing

This simple Asian dressing balances the creamy taste of pumpkin seeds with the sour snap of umeboshi plums, a type of Japanese pickle. Traditional recipes call for grinding the ingredients together by hand in a suribachi, a ribbed pottery bowl used as a mortar in Japan, but a blender is faster. Try the dressing over a salad of greens and tomatoes or tossed with warm noodles and diced carrots.

START TO FINISH: 5 MINUTES
Makes 1 cup

TIP: Pumpkin seeds can be bought roasted or raw. To dry roast raw seeds, wash under cool water in a mesh strainer. Transfer the seeds to a lightly oiled baking sheet and bake at 350°F 10 minutes or until the seeds begin to puff and lightly brown.

1 umeboshi plum (or ½ tablespoon umeboshi plum vinegar)

¼ cup dry-roasted pumpkin seeds

3–4 tablespoons water

2 scallions, with greens, finely chopped

Combine all ingredients in a blender and purée until smooth. Refrigerate dressing for up to 1 week. Bring it to room temperature before serving.

pesto

Fresh pesto, with its vibrant basil blended with luscious olive oil and ground pine nuts, is the perfect complement to fresh pasta and warm bread. In this version, nutritional yeast flakes, instead of Parmesan cheese, give the pesto its zing.

START TO FINISH: 10 MINUTES
Makes 1 cup

TIP: As an alternative to yeast flakes, you also can use an equal amount of a commercial soy Parmesan cheese. Alone these cheeses taste a bit fabricated, but they do well in recipes such as this.

Toss the pesto with warm pasta, drizzle it over hot soup or mix it with a bit of additional olive oil and dip fresh bread in it.

¼ cup raw pine nuts

2 cups packed fresh basil leaves

½ cup extra-virgin olive oil

2 tablespoons nutritional yeast flakes

2 cloves garlic

½ teaspoon sea salt

Toast the pine nuts in a dry skillet over a medium flame until just barely browned, about 4 minutes.

Combine all ingredients in a food processor or blender and purée until almost smooth. To store pesto, cover the top with a thin layer of olive oil and refrigerate.

sassy cranberry sauce

We are huge fans of cranberry sauce in all its varied forms, from the cans of jelly to whole-berry home-made versions. But this recipe beats them all. The crystallized ginger dissolves when cooked, accenting the sweetness of the pears and the tender bite of the cranberries. This can be made several days ahead of time. And don't save it just for Thanksgiving— serve with mashed potatoes and gravy any time.

START TO FINISH: 30 MINUTES

Makes about 3 cups

TIP: Toss a few tablespoons of this sauce with warm linguini and serve with an Italian red wine.

- 3 cups (12-ounce bag) fresh cranberries
- 3 cups chopped pears (about 2 medium pears)
- 1 cup orange or apple juice
- ½ cup dried, unsweetened cherries
- ½ cup golden raisins
- 1 cup sugar
- 3 tablespoons minced crystallized ginger (also called candied ginger)
- ⅛ teaspoon ground cardamom

Combine all ingredients in a large saucepan. Cover and bring to a gentle boil over a medium-low flame. Cook 12 minutes. Uncover, reduce heat to a simmer and cook until sauce thickens, about 5 minutes.

Transfer the sauce to a heat-proof bowl and cool 10 minutes. Cover and refrigerate at least 1 hour before serving.

sweet eggplant sauce

A friend once gave us a bottle of super-sweet passion fruit liqueur that tasted awful. It sat on the shelf a few years until inspiration hit. Now we have this incredible sauce that is equally good on crostini or mixed with steaming bowls of pasta.

START TO FINISH: 25 MINUTES

Makes 4 cups

TIP: The recipe calls for passion fruit liqueur, which is made in Portugal. We've had equal success with pineapple and other fruit liqueurs. If you can't find anything suitable, port wine also is good.

- 1 tablespoon extra-virgin olive oil
- 1 large onion, diced
- ½ teaspoon freshly ground black pepper
- 2 medium eggplants, peeled and diced
- 1½ teaspoons sea salt
- 2 cups passion fruit liqueur

Combine the olive oil, onion and pepper in a large skillet and sauté until the onion is soft, about 6 minutes.

Add the eggplant, salt and liqueur, and stir to coat. Cover and reduce the heat to medium-low. Cook 12 minutes or until the eggplant is tender and the liquid thick and syrupy.

basic bourbon baste

This basting sauce does double duty. It's great for marinating and grilling vegetables, tofu and tempeh but also is a good dipping sauce for California Sushi Rolls (recipe p. 17) and Fresh Spring Rolls (recipe p. 14).

START TO FINISH: 1 HOUR

Makes 1¼ cups

TIP: Use a large, heavy saucepan to let the sauce slow simmer and develop deep, concentrated flavors. Refrigerate in a covered container up to 2 weeks.

Instead of capers, substitute vegetarian Worcestershire sauce. Traditional Worcestershire sauces contain anchovies.

- 1 **cup soy sauce**
- ½ **cup bourbon**
- ¼ **cup water**
- ¼ **cup canola oil**
- 1 **tablespoon cider vinegar**
- 1 **tablespoon blackstrap molasses**
- 1 **tablespoon hot pepper sauce**
- ½ **tablespoon capers, crushed with a fork**
- 4 **cloves garlic, minced**
- 1 **teaspoon freshly ground ginger**
- **Pinch ground cloves**

Combine all ingredients in a medium saucepan and bring to a boil. Reduce heat to a simmer and cook 1 hour to reduce liquid by roughly half.

stick-to-your-ribs gravy

Try this gravy over Fluffy Biscuits (recipe p. 34), mashed or roasted potatoes or sautéed tofu or seitan. Even better, use it as a dip for bread hot from oven.

START TO FINISH: 30 MINUTES

Makes 2 cups

TIP: Don't like garlic? Substitute 1½ teaspoons grated fresh ginger, 1 tablespoon fresh minced parsley and 1 tablespoon fresh grated daikon radish.

- 8 **tablespoons extra-virgin olive oil**
- 5 **cloves garlic, crushed**
- ½ **medium yellow onion, diced**
- 1 **cup button mushrooms, thinly sliced**
- 5 **fresh sage leaves, cut into thin strips**
- 8 **tablespoons unbleached white flour**
- 2 **tablespoons nutritional yeast flakes**
- 4 **tablespoons soy sauce**
- 2 **cups water**
- ¼ **cup red wine**
- 2 **tablespoons balsamic vinegar**
- **Pinch sea salt**
- ½ **teaspoon freshly ground black pepper**

Combine the oil, garlic, onion, mushrooms and sage in a small saucepan. Heat over a medium-low flame and cook until the onion is soft, about 6 minutes.

Add the flour, yeast flakes and soy sauce, stirring constantly to make a paste. Gradually add the water, stirring constantly.

Bring to a boil and cook until the gravy thickens, 5–10 minutes. Add the red wine and vinegar and simmer another 5–10 minutes or until the gravy reaches desired thickness. Season with salt and pepper.

mushroom gravy

This gravy is outstanding on mashed potatoes, vegetarian "meatballs" or anything you'd be tempted to ladle gravy over.

START TO FINISH: 25 MINUTES

Makes 2 cups

TIP: For the mushroom mix, try a combination of white button, enoki, Portobello, lobster and shiitake.

> 2 cups diced yellow onions
>
> 2 cloves garlic, minced
>
> 1 tablespoon extra-virgin olive oil
>
> 2 cloves garlic, minced
>
> ½ teaspoon dried basil
>
> ½ teaspoon dried oregano
>
> ½ teaspoon dried thyme
>
> ½ teaspoon dried sage
>
> ½ teaspoon sea salt
>
> 1 teaspoon sesame oil
>
> 4 teaspoons nutritional yeast flakes
>
> 2½ cups diced mushrooms
> (any variety or a mix)
>
> 2 tablespoons soy sauce
>
> 1½ cups plain rice milk or soy milk
>
> 1 cup vegetable stock or water
>
> 4 tablespoons unbleached white flour
> or whole wheat pastry flour
>
> 2 tablespoons soy margarine

In a medium saucepan, sauté the onions and garlic in the olive oil over medium-high flame until soft, about 6 minutes. Add the herbs and salt, then cook an additional minute, stirring frequently. Add the sesame oil, yeast flakes, mushrooms, soy sauce, rice milk and vegetable stock or water. Simmer 2 minutes. Set aside.

Heat a large skillet over a medium-high flame. Add the flour and lightly toast, stirring constantly, until just barely brown. Transfer flour to a small bowl.

Return the skillet to the heat and melt the margarine. Sprinkle the toasted flour into the pan, stirring constantly. Cook until the mixture, called a roux, thickens.

Ladle about ½ cup of the liquid from the mushroom mixture into the skillet, stirring constantly until thickened. Repeat with an additional ½ cup of liquid.

Add the remaining mushroom mixture to the skillet and simmer until heated through and thick, stirring constantly. Simmer an additional 5 minutes.

desserts and snacks

carrot cake

½ cup golden raisins

2 cups unbleached white flour

1 cup whole wheat pastry flour

1 tablespoon baking powder

2 teaspoons baking soda

1 teaspoon sea salt

1 teaspoon allspice

1 teaspoon nutmeg

2 teaspoons cinnamon

¾ cup corn oil

½ cup maple syrup

¼ cup brown rice syrup or additional maple syrup

¼ cup blackstrap molasses

½ cup vanilla rice milk

⅓ cup apple sauce

1 tablespoon vanilla extract

3 ½ cups finely grated carrots

2 tablespoons cider vinegar

START TO FINISH:
1 ½ hours
Makes 8–10 slices

TIP: A standing mixer makes this recipe even easier. If you are mixing by hand, it is best to add the ingredients one at a time rather than all at once, as called for in the directions.

Preheat the oven to 350°F. Lightly oil a standard (10-inch) bundt pan.

Place the raisins in a small bowl and cover with warm water. Let stand 20 minutes to soften. Drain and set aside.

Meanwhile, combine all remaining ingredients except the vinegar in a large mixing bow. Mix until combined.

Mix the raisins into the batter. Add the vinegar and mix again. Batter may begin to bubble.

Spoon the batter into the prepared pan and smooth the top. Bake 45–60 minutes or until the edges of the cake pull away from the pan and a toothpick inserted into the center comes out clean.

Let the cake cool 10 minutes in the pan. Run a knife along the edges to separate the cake from the pan. Turn the cake out onto a wire cooling rack.

best chocolate cake

The wonderfully talented chefs at Cook's Illustrated *magazine test recipes hundreds of times until they get them just right. Challenged by J.M. to create the best dairy-free chocolate cake, they spent months baking countless cakes until they were satisfied that their recipe tasted as good as a conventional one. Though this was their first venture into vegan territory, the cooks at* Cook's *managed brilliantly. This cake is incredible. Try it with the Creamy Chocolate Frosting (recipe follows) the test chefs whipped up to go with it.*

1⅔	cups natural large-crystal cane sugar
2½	cups all-purpose flour
½	cup oat flour
2	teaspoons baking soda
¾	teaspoon sea salt
⅓	cup Dutch-processed cocoa
⅓	cup natural cocoa
1½	ounces unsweetened chocolate, chopped
1	cup hot brewed coffee
1	cup light coconut milk
2	tablespoons cider or white wine vinegar
1½	teaspoons vanilla extract
¾	cup vegan butter substitute

Preheat oven to 350°F. Adjust oven rack to the middle position. Lightly oil two 9-inch round cake pans.

Process the sugar in a food processor to a fine powder, 30–40 seconds. Sift sugar, flours, baking soda and salt into a large bowl, then whisk to combine.

In a large bowl, combine the cocoas and chocolate. Whisk in the hot coffee until the chocolate melts and is smooth.

In a large measuring cup, combine the coconut milk, cider and vanilla. Place the vegan butter substitute in a medium bowl. Add the coconut milk mixture in two batches, whisking until smooth after each.

Add vegan butter-coconut milk mixture to the chocolate mixture and whisk to combine, then add this mixture to the dry ingredients and fold gently with a rubber spatula until just incorporated and no streaks of flour remain.

Divide the batter evenly between cake pans and bake until a toothpick inserted in center comes out clean, 20–25 minutes, switching the position of the pans and rotating them after 12 minutes. Cool the cakes in the pans on a wire rack to room temperature, about 2 hours.

TO FROST THE CAKE:

Invert the cakes from their pans. Spread a dab of frosting in the center of a cardboard round cut slightly larger than the cake. Place one cake, centered, on the cardboard round. The frosting helps hold it in place.

Using an icing spatula, spread about 1 cup frosting evenly onto the top of the first cake. Place the second cake on top of frosted bottom layer and spread about 1 cup frosting on top. Cover sides of cake with remaining frosting.

creamy chocolate frosting

Two 10-ounce packages vegan or other semisweet chocolate chips
½ cup hot brewed coffee
4 tablespoons boiling water
½ cup light coconut milk
4 ounces silken tofu

Bring 1 inch of water to a simmer in the bottom half of a double boiler. Add the chocolate chips to the upper part of the boiler. Remove from the heat, add the coffee and water and whisk until chocolate is smooth. Whisk in the coconut milk until incorporated.

Combine the chocolate mixture and tofu in a food processor and process until smooth, about 10–15 seconds, scraping down the bowl once or twice.

Transfer the mixture to a medium bowl and cover with plastic wrap. Refrigerate until cool and texture resembles firm cream cheese, about 1½ hours. (If mixture has chilled for longer and is very stiff, let stand at room temperature 1 hour.)

Transfer the cooled chocolate mixture to the bowl of a standing mixer fitted with a whisk attachment. Whip the mixture at high speed until fluffy and mousse-like and the mixture forms medium stiff peaks, about 1½ minutes.

START TO FINISH:
1½ hours
(10 minutes active)
Makes about 3 cups

TIP: *Cook's Illustrated tested specific brand ingredients. They preferred Tropical Source dairy-free chocolate chips.*

name-your-fruit coffee cake

Throw together this great brunch cake in no time. It can also double as a dessert served warm with soy "ice cream."

Just about any fruit will do. We like blueberries, but raspberries or apples are great, too. If you decide to use apples, we suggest making the apple pie filling (recipe p. 170).

1½ cups fresh or frozen fruit

¼ cup water

1 cup maple syrup crystals or sugar

2 tablespoons arrowroot or cornstarch

1¾ cups unbleached white flour

½ teaspoon baking powder

¼ teaspoon baking soda

6 tablespoons soy margarine

1 egg's worth of powdered egg replacer (prepared with water according to package directions)

¾ cup vanilla rice milk

½ teaspoon cider vinegar

½ teaspoon vanilla extract

Preheat the oven to 350°F. Lightly oil an 8 × 8-inch cake pan.

Combine the fruit and water in a medium saucepan and bring to a boil. Reduce the heat, cover and simmer about 5 minutes. In a small bowl, combine ¼ cup maple syrup crystals and the arrowroot. Stir the mixture into the fruit. Simmer, uncovered, until fruit is thick, 3–4 minutes. Set aside.

In a mixing bowl, combine ½ cup maple syrup crystals, 1½ cups flour, baking powder and baking soda. Cut in 4 tablespoons margarine until the mixture resembles fine crumbs.

In a small bowl, combine the egg replacer, rice milk, vinegar and vanilla. Add to the flour mixture and stir until just combined. Spread half the batter into the baking dish. Spread the fruit mixture over the batter. Drop the remaining batter by small spoonfuls over the fruit.

Combine the remaining ¼ cup maple syrup crystals and ¼ cup flour in a small bowl. Cut in the remaining 2 tablespoons margarine until the mixture resembles fine crumbs. Sprinkle over the top layer of batter.

Bake 40–45 minutes or until the top is golden brown. Cool and cut into squares.

START TO FINISH:

1 hour

Makes 1 8 × 8-inch square cake, 9 servings

TIP: When baking instructions call for a lightly oiled pan, corn oil is best. It gives baked goods a buttery flavor. Cut any fruit larger than a small berry into ⅓-inch chunks to ensure even baking.

Powdered egg replacers are available at most natural food stores. They contain a variety of starches that bind together ingredients in baked goods, much as eggs would.

oatmeal-raisin chocolate chip cookies

This recipe has everything we love in a tender, chewy cookie—oats, brown sugar, raisins, chocolate chips and traditional baking spices. These cookies have been a family favorite for more than 30 years.

2	**cups unbleached all-purpose white flour**
½	**teaspoon sea salt**
½	**teaspoon baking soda**
½	**teaspoon baking powder**
1	**teaspoon cinnamon**
½	**teaspoon ground cloves**
1	**cup natural shortening**
1½	**cups brown sugar**
	Powdered egg replacer equivalent to 2 eggs
⅔	**cup plain soy milk**
1	**teaspoon lemon juice**
1½	**cups rolled oats**
1	**cup raisins**
1	**cup dark chocolate chips** *or* **other nondairy chocolate chips**

Preheat the oven to 350°F. Lightly oil a baking sheet.

In a medium bowl, sift together the flour, salt, baking soda, baking powder and spices. Set aside.

Using a standing or hand-held mixer, beat the shortening and brown sugar together until fluffy. Add the egg replacer (without reconstituting) and mix. Add the dry ingredients and beat until mixed.

In a separate bowl, combine the soy milk, lemon juice and any water called for by the egg replacer instructions.

A bit at a time, add the liquid to the flour mixture and mix. Add the oats, raisins and chocolate chips and mix.

Drop teaspoon-sized balls of dough onto the prepared baking sheet. Bake 12–15 minutes or until lightly browned. Cool the cookies 1 minute on the baking sheet. Transfer the cookies to a wire rack to cool completely.

joe frogger's cookies

These cookies are great around the holidays (is there a bad time for cookies?).

4⅓	cups unbleached white flour
1	teaspoon baking soda
½	teaspoon sea salt
1½	teaspoons powdered ginger
¾	teaspoon ground cloves
¾	teaspoon nutmeg
¼	teaspoon allspice
¾	cup natural shortening
⅔	cup maple syrup
⅔	cup molasses
1	teaspoon rum extract
¼	cup water
1	teaspoon corn oil

In a large bowl, combine the flour, baking soda, salt and spices.

In a separate bowl, cream the shortening and maple syrup. Fold in the flour mixture. Add the molasses, rum extract and water, and mix.

Cover the bowl with plastic wrap. Chill 1 hour.

Preheat the oven to 350°F. Lightly coat a baking sheet with the oil.

Divide the dough in half. Leave one half in the refrigerator. Roll out the other half to ¼ inch thickness on a lightly floured surface.

Cut circles out of the dough with a 4-inch cookie cutter. Place the cookies on the prepared baking sheet and bake until golden, about 12 minutes. Repeat with second half of dough.

START TO FINISH:
1½ hours
(15 minutes active)
Makes 12–16 cookies

TIP: Be sure to keep a close eye on the cookies during the final 5 minutes of baking, as they can easily overcook and become dry and brittle.

no-bake apple pie

It's hard to imagine an apple pie can be this easy and still taste so good. In the summer, serve it chilled with a glass of crisp dessert wine or light fruit juice. In the fall and winter, warm it up and serve it topped with a dollop of nondairy vanilla "ice cream."

If you like a bit more tooth to your apple pies, reduce the dried apples by about a third and add the same amount of chopped fresh apples during the final 5–10 minutes of simmering, depending on how tender you want the apple chunks.

1 **9-inch Basic Pie Crust, pre-baked (recipe follows)**
½ **pound dried apple chunks**
   Water to cover
1 **teaspoon cinnamon**
3 **tablespoons brown rice syrup or maple syrup**
½ **tablespoon kuzu**

Place the apples in a medium saucepan and add enough water to cover by about ½ inch. Let stand 15 minutes.

Add cinnamon and brown rice syrup to the apples and simmer about 15 minutes or until the liquid turns syrupy and the apples are tender. Add another ½ cup water if needed.

In a glass, mix the kuzu with 1/4 cup cold water. Stir the kuzu mixture into the apple mixture. Continue simmering until the mixture thickens, 3–4 minutes. Pour the apple mixture into the pie crust and refrigerate about 2 hours.

START TO FINISH:
2 hours, 40 minutes
(30 minutes active)
Makes 1 9-inch pie

TIP: Natural food stores sell wonderful prepared pie crusts that you just pop in the oven and bake. Or try a simple gingersnap crust. Use a food processor to finely chop 3 handfuls of gingersnaps. Melt 6 tablespoons soy margarine and add to the gingersnap crumbs. Pulse until crumbs form a loose, clumpy mixture. Press this mixture into a pie plate and bake at 350°F 10 minutes or until just beginning to brown. Cool completely before filling.

basic pie crust

Use this pie crust for just about anything. It's sweet enough for desserts but not so sweet that it can't do double duty as a crust for a savory vegetable pot pie.

½   **cup whole wheat pastry flour**

½   **cup unbleached white flour**

⅛   **teaspoon sea salt**

    Pinch cinnamon (optional)

14   **tablespoons (1¾ sticks) soy margarine, chilled and cut into small chunks**

2   **tablespoons brown rice syrup *or* maple syrup**

¼   **cup apple juice *or* soy milk *or* water**

Preheat the oven to 350°F. Lightly oil a 9-inch pie pan.

In the bowl of a food processor, combine the flours and salt (and cinnamon, if desired). While pulsing, add the margarine until the mixture resembles a coarse meal.

Continue pulsing, adding the brown rice syrup and 1 tablespoon of apple juice. Add additional juice a bit at a time until the dough forms a soft ball.

Turn the dough out onto a lightly floured surface and form into a flattened disk. Dough will look marbled.

Lightly flour the top and bottom of the dough and place between two sheets of waxed paper or parchment. Roll out the dough into a 12-inch circle.

Remove the top sheet of waxed paper. Place the prepared pan upside down on the crust. Placing one hand under the crust and one on top of the pie plate, invert the plate so the crust is within.

Peel off the remaining waxed paper.

Fold over the excess crust and crimp to form a rim. Bake 12–15 minutes or until just golden brown. Remove from the oven and cool.

START TO FINISH:
25 minutes
Makes 1 9-inch
pie crust

TIP: Making pie shells can be a pain. Save yourself some trouble and make several at a time. Buy disposable pie plates and line them with the unbaked crusts. Instead of baking, cover tightly with plastic wrap and freeze. When you need a pie shell, just thaw and bake.

chocolate fudge pie

This pie's combination of cashew butter—by far the richest of all nut butters—chocolate chips and cocoa powder is heavenly. Think creamy smooth, buttery fudge with a mousse-like consistency.

	12-ounce package soft, silken tofu
1	cup cashew nut butter
1	teaspoon vanilla
1	tablespoon cocoa powder
⅛	teaspoon cinnamon
2	cups (about 1 bag) dark *or* nondairy chocolate chips
	9-inch Basic Pie Crust, pre-baked (recipe p. 171)

Combine the tofu, cashew butter, vanilla, cocoa powder and cinnamon in a food processor and purée until smooth. Scrape down the sides of the processor bowl as needed. Set aside, leaving the tofu mixture in the food processor.

Bring several cups of water to a boil in the bottom half of a double boiler. Add the chocolate chips to the upper part of the boiler. Remove boiler from the heat. Stir until the chips melt, about 2 minutes.

Add the melted chocolate to the tofu mixture and pulse to combine.

Pour the filling into the pie crust and smooth the top. Chill the pie in the refrigerator 2–3 hours before serving.

**START TO FINISH:
10 minutes to prepare,
about 2 hours chilling
Makes 1 9-inch pie**

TIP: When melting chocolate chips in a double boiler, don't leave the burner on too long. Bring the water to a boil, then turn off the heat. The residual heat will melt the chips. Too much heat scorches the chocolate. Also be careful of getting any water in the chocolate; even a drop can ruin the consistency.

Dark chocolate is naturally dairy-free, but be sure to read labels.

sweet and spicy loaf

The blend of sweet and spicy in this loaf makes it a great light dessert, or a luscious accompaniment to soup.

START TO FINISH:

1½ hours

Makes 1 9 × 5-inch loaf

TIP: This loaf freezes well, especially when sliced and packaged in individual plastic bags. Frozen slices packed in lunch boxes will be thawed by noon.

1	teaspoon corn oil, plus 1 tablespoon
1	cup whole wheat pastry flour
¼	cup oat flour
¼	cup cornmeal
1	teaspoon baking soda
¾	teaspoon baking powder
1	teaspoon powdered ginger
½	teaspoon cinnamon
½	teaspoon nutmeg
1	cup canned pumpkin
½	cup maple syrup
1½	tablespoons barley malt syrup *or* molasses
¼	cup water
¼	cup prune purée or apple sauce
1	teaspoon cider vinegar
¼	cup golden raisins
¼	cup chopped candied ginger

Preheat the oven to 325°F. Lightly coat a standard 9 × 5-inch loaf pan with 1 teaspoon oil.

In a medium bowl, sift together the pastry flour, oat flour, cornmeal, baking soda, baking powder, ginger, cinnamon and nutmeg. Set aside.

In a large bowl, whisk together the pumpkin, maple and barley malt syrups, water, prune purée, remaining oil and vinegar until smooth.

Add the dry ingredients to the wet mixture and mix until just combined. Add the raisins and ginger and mix to combine.

Pour the batter into the prepared loaf pan. Bake 1¼ hours or until a toothpick inserted into the center of the loaf comes out clean.

Cool 10 minutes before slicing.

gingerbread

This aromatic bread is just sweet enough for dessert but just dry and light enough to accompany a plate of mashed potatoes, roasted vegetables and a hearty soup.

For a richer version, soak 1 cup golden raisins in 1 cup warm water and 1 cup rum 20 minutes. Drain the raisins and add to the batter at the same time as the flour and other ingredients. Use ⅔ cup of the soaking liquid as the water for the batter.

¼ cup corn oil

¼ cup soft, silken tofu

2¼ cups whole wheat pastry flour

½ teaspoon sea salt

2 tablespoons brown rice syrup or maple syrup

⅓ cup applesauce

1 teaspoon baking soda

⅔ cup blackstrap molasses

½ teaspoon powdered ginger

1½ teaspoons fresh ginger juice (from the gratings of a 1½-inch piece of ginger)

1 teaspoon cinnamon

⅔ cup warm water

1 teaspoon cider vinegar

Preheat the oven to 350°F. Lightly oil a standard 9 × 5-inch loaf pan.

Combine oil and tofu in a blender and purée until smooth. Set aside.

In a large mixing bowl, combine the tofu mixture and all remaining ingredients except the vinegar. Mix until smooth.

Quickly mix the vinegar into the batter. Transfer the batter to the prepared loaf pan. Bake 45 minutes or until a toothpick inserted in the center comes out clean.

Allow the bread to cool 5 minutes before removing it from the pan. Cool another 20 minutes before slicing.

START TO FINISH:
1 hour
Makes 1 9 × 5-inch loaf

TIP: To make fresh ginger juice, grate a large piece of ginger over a fine grater placed over a bowl. Grab the shavings with your fingers and squeeze out the juice.

A good substitute for molasses is barley malt syrup. Use an equal amount.

baked apples

This minimalist dessert packs a wallop. It's simple, yet sweet and satisfying.
Try it plain, or wrapped in a crepe and topped with vanilla soy "ice cream."

START TO FINISH:

30 minutes

Makes 4 servings

TIP: Bake this dessert
shortly before eating.
But you can do some of
the work ahead. Cut
the apples and peaches,
then place them in a
medium bowl and splash
with orange juice. The
acid in the juice will
keep them from turning
brown. Drain well before
using.

8	medium apples, cored and sliced into half-moons
3	peaches, pitted and sliced into half-moons
1	cup maple syrup crystals or sugar
½	cup corn oil
1	teaspoon cinnamon
	Pinch nutmeg
½	teaspoon vanilla
½	cup honey liqueur *or* other sweet dessert wine
¼	cup chopped mixed nuts, lightly toasted

Preheat the oven to 375°F.

Combine the apples and peaches in a large baking dish. In a small bowl, whisk together ½ cup of the maple syrup crystals or sugar, ¼ cup of the oil, cinnamon, nutmeg and vanilla. Pour the mixture over the fruit. Bake 5 minutes. Set aside.

Meanwhile, combine the remaining sugar and oil in a small saucepan. Simmer until the sugar caramelizes, 2–3 minutes.

Sprinkle liqueur evenly over the baked fruit. Pour the warm sugar mixture over the fruit. Return the baking dish to the oven another 15 minutes or until the apples are tender. Just before serving, sprinkle with chopped nuts.

chocolate truffles

In this recipe tofu and nuts replicate the creamy fullness so important to chocolate dishes that is often provided by cream, butter and eggs. It comes to us via Catriona May, a wonderful chocoholic and vegan chef from Glasgow, Scotland.

- ¼ cup maple syrup
- 1 cup almonds, dry-roasted
- 1 12-ounce package soft, silken tofu
- 2 cups dark or nondairy chocolate chips
- ½ cup cocoa powder, for garnish
- ½ cup crushed almonds, for garnish

In a saucepan, bring maple syrup to a boil over a medium flame. Add the dry-roasted almonds and stir until the mixture thickens, 12–14 minutes.

Spread the almond mixture on waxed paper to cool and harden. Once hardened, break into pieces and process in a food processor until the mixture resembles a coarse flour. Set aside.

Process the tofu in the food processor until smooth. Set aside.

Bring several cups of water to a boil in the bottom half of a double boiler. Add the chocolate chips to the upper part of the boiler. Remove from the heat and stir until the chips melt, about 2 minutes.

In a bowl, combine the chocolate and nut mixture. Fold in the tofu.

Spread the mixture in a lightly oiled shallow baking dish and refrigerate 2 hours or until firm. Using a sturdy teaspoon or melon baller, scoop out mixture and form into small balls.

Roll each ball in either the crushed almonds or cocoa powder. Truffles can be stored in the refrigerator for up to 2 weeks.

START TO FINISH: 4 hours (20 minutes active) Makes 25–30 truffles

TIP: If dairy allergies are a concern, read the labels carefully. Many chocolate makers use the same machines to make milk and dark chocolates and warn that their dairy-free versions can contain trace amounts of dairy products.

The colder the mixture (prior to scooping out and rolling into balls) the better. In fact, after chilling it helps to put the mixture in a freezer 15 minutes immediately before making the truffle balls. Expect to make a mess; the chocolate will get all over you. But the end result will be well worth it.

frozen fudge pops

The switch to a dairy-free diet too often means ultimate summer comfort foods such as ice cream and fudge pops are either off-limits or replaced with icy, tasteless variations. But a little effort and a bit of tofu (even against our better judgment) can make creamy frozen treats that taste as good as the real thing.

	12-ounce package soft, silken tofu
3	tablespoons cocoa powder
3	tablespoons maple syrup
1½	cups dark or nondairy chocolate chips

Process the tofu in a food processor until smooth, about 1 minute. Scrape down the sides of the bowl and purée another minute. The tofu should look creamy smooth, like yogurt.

Add the cocoa and purée another minute. Scrape down the sides and repeat. Add the maple syrup and purée 1 minute. Scrape down the sides and repeat.

Bring several cups of water to a boil in the bottom half of a double boiler. Add the chocolate chips to the upper part of the boiler. Remove from the heat. Stir until the chips melt, about 2 minutes.

Pour the melted chocolate into the food processor and purée 3 minutes, scraping down the sides of the processor bowl a few times. Pour the mixture into the molds and top with sticks or handles. Freeze about 3 hours.

START TO FINISH: 3 hours
(10 minutes active)
Makes 6 servings
(depending on size of molds)

TIP: It is very important to use soft, silken tofu. Other grades of tofu won't purée completely, no matter how long they're mixed.

Inexpensive frozen pop molds are easy to find. But getting the pops out of them can be a challenge. Run the mold under warm water a few seconds to loosen the pop.

chocolate-cherry rice pudding

This rice pudding is easy to make, creamy and reminds us of chocolate-covered cherries.

1½   **cups short-grain white rice, such as Arborio**

2   **cups water**

1   **cup maple syrup**

4   **cups vanilla soy milk**

1   **teaspoon lemon juice**

½   **teaspoon sea salt**

⅓   **cup cocoa powder**

  Pinch cinnamon

½   **cup dried cherries**

Preheat the oven to 325°F. Rinse the rice in a mesh strainer and set aside to drain.

Combine the water, maple syrup, soy milk, lemon juice, salt, cocoa and cinnamon in a medium oven-proof saucepan. Bring to a boil over medium-high flame, stirring occasionally.

Add the rice and cherries. Remove from the heat and cover the saucepan. Place the saucepan in the oven and bake 1 hour. Serve warm or chilled.

corn and maple rice pudding

Rice pudding is one of the best comfort foods. So rich, it goes down great warm or cold.

2 cups Arborio rice

6 cups vanilla rice milk

⅔ cup maple syrup

1 teaspoon vanilla

3 cups corn kernels

2 tablespoons grated fresh ginger

Pinch sea salt

¼ cup sweet white wine (Moscato is good)

½ cup golden raisins

Rinse the rice in a mesh strainer under cool water and drain. Combine the rice, rice milk and maple syrup in a large saucepan over a medium flame. Bring to a boil, then reduce to a simmer. Cover and cook until most of the milk is absorbed, about 30 minutes.

Stir in the vanilla, corn, ginger, salt, wine and 1/4 cup of raisins. Cook over a low flame until thick and pudding-like, 5–10 minutes. Stir frequently to prevent sticking.

Garnish with remaining raisins and serve warm or cool.

START TO FINISH:
45 minutes
Makes 4–6 servings

TIP: To leave out the wine, substitute an equal amount of apple juice. For a twist, add pinches of cinnamon and nutmeg during simmering.

banana "butterscotch" pudding

When we gave up dairy, we figured butterscotch pudding was a goner. But thanks to some creative playing with soy margarine and sugar, this dessert has been resurrected.

Use this either as the filling for a pre-baked pie shell or on its own.

START TO FINISH:

2½ hours

(25 minutes active)

Makes filling for

1 9-inch pie

TIP: We like to buy extra bananas, then peel and freeze them so we always have them on hand for recipes like this or for smoothies. Freeze each banana in a separate plastic bag or wrapped in foil, otherwise they will stick together.

- ¼ cup soft, silken tofu
- 2 cups vanilla soy milk
- 2 medium bananas, thinly sliced
- 2 tablespoons soy margarine
- ½ cup sugar
- ⅓ teaspoon sea salt
- 1 teaspoon vanilla extract
- 2 teaspoons kuzu
- 2 tablespoons water

Combine the tofu, soy milk and banana slices in a blender and purée until smooth. Transfer mixture to a medium saucepan and bring to a simmer.

In a small saucepan, combine the margarine and sugar over a low flame. Cook, stirring constantly, until the sugar and margarine melt and thicken, 6–8 minutes.

Slowly whisk in the soy milk mixture. Simmer 3–4 minutes or until the sugar is dissolved. Add the salt and vanilla and continue simmering, stirring, 2 minutes.

In a small glass, combine the kuzu with the water. Add to the pudding while stirring. Continue simmering until the pudding thickens, 3–5 minutes.

Pour the pudding into a pie shell or individual cups or ramekins and chill 2–3 hours.

chocolate pudding

Instant pudding need not come from a box. And dairy-free chocolate pudding need not taste like the box. This is great over warm brownies or vanilla soy "ice cream."

1½	cups dark or nondairy chocolate chips
Two	12-ounce packages soft, silken tofu
¼	cup safflower oil or walnut oil
4	tablespoons cocoa powder
¼	teaspoon sea salt
1½	teaspoons vanilla extract
½	cup sugar

Bring 1 inch of water to a boil in the bottom half of a double boiler. Add the chocolate chips to the top half and remove double boiler from the heat. Stir 2 minutes or until chips have melted.

Combine all the ingredients except the chocolate in a blender or food processor and purée until smooth. Add the chocolate and purée again until smooth. Serve immediately or chill.

START TO FINISH:
15 minutes
Makes 4 servings

TIP: Other oils that have either little taste, such as canola, or a predominantly buttery flavor, such as corn, also can be used. Avoid olive, sesame or peanut oils because their flavors are more pronounced.

vanilla pudding

You don't need milk and cream to make a creamy vanilla pudding.

START TO FINISH:

2 hours, 15 minutes
(15 minutes active)
Makes 4 servings

TIP: Vanilla soy milk gives this recipe extra flavor. Though soy and rice milk often are interchangeable, this isn't one of those cases. Rice milk is too thin to produce the creamy consistency desired here.

1	quart vanilla soy milk
½	cup maple syrup
4	tablespoons agar flakes
¼	teaspoon sea salt
1	teaspoon vanilla extract
¼	teaspoon nutmeg

Whisk together the soy milk, maple syrup, agar and salt in a large saucepan over a medium flame.

Bring to a boil, stirring occasionally. Reduce the heat and simmer about 5 minutes, stirring occasionally. Remove from heat and stir in vanilla and nutmeg.

Transfer pudding to a serving bowl or individual cups and chill 2 hours.

peach and berry kanten

If you like gelatin, you will love kanten. Agar, a plant-based jelling agent, works with any combination of fruits and juices, so use this recipe as a guide and make your own combinations.

½ cup sliced peaches

½ cup raspberries

2 cups apple juice

   Pinch sea salt

2 tablespoons agar flakes

1 tablespoon lemon juice

Arrange the peaches and berries in a medium bowl or mold. Combine the juice, salt and agar in a medium saucepan and bring to a boil.

Reduce the heat to a simmer and cook 5–8 minutes or until agar dissolves. Add the lemon juice and stir. Pour the agar mixture over the fruit. Let stand, in or out of the refrigerator, until cool and firm.

START TO FINISH:

2 hours

(15 minutes active)

Makes 4 servings

TIP: Agar typically comes in flakes and powders. Though we're sure some people are able to use both successfully, we've never had much luck with the powder, which is far more concentrated than the flakes. Whenever we've used it, our dishes come out like rubber balls. Stick with the flakes.

cheesy popcorn

This snack is proof that eating healthy doesn't mean you can't have fun. Bag this treat and bring it to the movies. This popcorn has a strong salty-cheesy flavor.

Popped corn

Nutritional yeast flakes

Soy sauce

EQUIPMENT:

Small spray bottle

Wooden spoon

While the corn is popping, pour the soy sauce into the spray bottle. As soon as the corn is popped, transfer it to a large mixing bowl (the larger the better).

Toss the popcorn with the wooden spoon while misting it with soy sauce.

Once most of the popcorn has been misted (be careful not to overspray and make the popcorn soggy), quickly begin dusting the popcorn with the yeast flakes.

Continue tossing the popcorn with the spoon while adding the yeast. Add flakes until the popcorn is lightly coated.

TIP: We haven't included amounts for this recipe because everyone seems to like different proportions. We suggest starting with a heaping bowl of popcorn and slowly adding the soy sauce and yeast flakes until you reach the taste you like. For each cup of unpopped corn, expect to use half as much yeast and 2 tablespoons of soy sauce.

Some nutritional yeast comes as large flakes. Toss it in a blender first to make a powder, which more evenly coats the popcorn.

stellar crispy bars

Good energy bars that aren't packed with processed ingredients and tons of sugar can be hard to find. Though we know it's bad to substitute a bar for a meal, we also live in the real world and sometimes this is as good a meal as you are likely to get.

1	tablespoon flax seeds
½	cup soy nuts, roasted, not salted
¾	cup rolled oats
3	cups puffed rice cereal
1	cup brown rice syrup or maple syrup
½	cup peanut butter
1	cup dark or dairy-free chocolate chips

Grind the flax seeds in a food processor or blender. Add the soy nuts and grind again. Add the oats and grind lightly. Transfer the mixture to a bowl. Stir in the puffed rice.

In a saucepan, melt the rice syrup and peanut butter over a medium flame. Stir the mixture into the dry ingredients.

Rinse a 9 × 13-inch baking pan with water but do not dry. With wet hands, pat the seed and oat mixture evenly into the pan, smoothing the top. Refrigerate to cool and harden, about 1 hour. When hard, cut into squares.

Bring several cups of water to a boil in the bottom half of a double boiler. Add the chocolate chips to the upper part of the boiler. Remove the pan from the heat. Stir the chips until they melt, 2–3 minutes.

Dip the top of each square into the melted chocolate. Place each bar, chocolate side up, on a baking sheet lined with waxed paper. Allow chocolate to cool and harden.

START TO FINISH:
10 minutes preparation, 1 hour chilling
Makes 12 bars

TIP: The beneficial oils in flax seeds don't tolerate warmth well. Always store flax seeds, whole or ground, in sealed jars in the refrigerator or freezer.

These bars store well in the freezer.

trifle

This gorgeous dessert can be made in about the same time it takes to bake a cake. It looks spectacular served in a clear glass bowl or trifle dish.

1   **Best Chocolate Cake (recipe p. 164)**

½   **cup all-fruit raspberry jam**

Vanilla Pudding (recipe p. 184) and/or Chocolate Pudding (recipe p. 183)

1   **cup sliced fruit**

½   **cup slivered almonds, for garnish (optional)**

After baking, remove the cake from the pan and cool completely. Cut the cake in half horizontally to make two layers.

Spread the jam over the bottom layer, then replace the cake's top layer, cut side down. Cut the cake into 1½- to 2-inch cubes.

Spoon some pudding over the bottom of the serving bowl. Place a layer of cake cubes over the pudding.

Top the cake cubes with a layer of pudding (if using chocolate and vanilla, alternate flavors as you go). Repeat layering until all ingredients are used, ending with a layer of pudding.

Cover and refrigerate 1 hour before serving.

Just before serving, decorate the top with fruit and nuts.

START TO FINISH:

1½ hours

Makes 6–8 servings

TIP: Use either the vanilla or chocolate pudding recipes, or get creative and use both. We like lots of pudding in our trifle, so we usually double the recipe. This also looks great as individual servings in parfait glasses.

breakfast

black bean and potato hash

This also is wonderful as a quick mid-week dinner. Serve with flatbread (recipe p. 29) and avocado slices.

(recipe p. 29)

START TO FINISH:

30 minutes

Makes 2–4 servings

TIP: To reduce the cooking time of this dish, bake or steam the potatoes ahead of time. Strain the tomatoes to reduce the liquid, then cook until warm, about 5 minutes.

1   pound Yukon gold potatoes, diced to ¼-inch chunks

1   medium yellow onion, diced

3   tablespoons extra-virgin olive oil

1   green bell pepper, seeded and diced

   14½-ounce can diced tomatoes, drained

   15-ounce can black beans, drained and rinsed

1   tablespoon nutritional yeast flakes

1   teaspoon dried oregano

¼   teaspoon paprika

   Sea salt and freshly ground black pepper, to taste

Preheat the oven to 400°F.

Combine the potatoes, onion and 2 tablespoons of oil in a large bowl and toss to coat evenly. Transfer potatoes and onion to a baking sheet and roast 20 minutes or until potatoes just begin to brown. Broil another 2 minutes to crisp.

In a large skillet, combine remaining oil and bell pepper and sauté over a medium flame 5 minutes or until pepper is tender.

Lower heat and add the tomatoes and beans. Sauté 3–5 minutes or until warm. Add yeast flakes, oregano, paprika, potatoes and onion and toss to combine. Season with salt and pepper to taste.

spare-the-pigs hash

We're usually pretty brave about trying new recipes on unsuspecting guests. But for this one, we were a bit concerned. We had taken a recipe that called for just about everything we don't eat, from smoked salmon to sour cream and butter. Worse yet, we didn't give much thought as to how we would "improve" the recipe. We just randomly assigned new ingredients. But we did something right. A picky crowd pecked away at it, and then asked for more.

START TO FINISH:
30 minutes
Makes 6 servings

TIP: Use frozen hash browns to speed up this recipe. Skip directly to the step that calls for combining the potatoes and oil in a large skillet.

- 1 **pound Russet potatoes**
- 3 **tablespoons extra-virgin olive oil**
- 2 **teaspoons sea salt**
- 1 **teaspoon freshly ground black pepper**
- 12 **ounces soy or tempeh bacon, cut into ½-inch squares**
- 1½ **cups minced scallions**
- 3 **tablespoons capers**
- 3 **tablespoons soy sour cream (an equal amount of soy yogurt plus 1 tablespoon white or cider vinegar can be substituted)**
- 2 **tablespoons wasabi powder**
- 1 **tablespoon whole-grain Dijon mustard**

Bring about 1 inch of water to a boil in a pot fitted with a steamer basket.

Using a grater or food processor, cut the potatoes into fine matchsticks.

Steam the potatoes 8 minutes or until just tender. Remove from the steamer basket and drip dry potatoes 5 minutes.

Combine the oil and potatoes in a large skillet and sauté over a medium-high flame until the potatoes begin to brown, about 8 minutes. Season with salt and pepper.

Meanwhile, combine all remaining ingredients in a medium bowl. Add the bacon and sour cream mixture to the browned potatoes and cook just long enough to heat, about 3 minutes.

blueberry muffins

After switching to a healthy diet, we went years without a good blueberry muffin. Dairy- and egg-free muffins usually are dull and dry.

One day we found a recipe that purported to make the "best" blueberry muffins. Of course it was loaded with butter, eggs and sour cream.

With the help of a little powdered egg replacer, soy yogurt and corn oil, the best got even better—better for you.

START TO FINISH:

45 minutes

Makes 12 muffins

2 cups unbleached white flour

1 tablespoon baking powder

½ teaspoon sea salt

Egg replacer, equivalent to 1 egg (follow package directions)

4 tablespoons corn oil

1¼ cups soy yogurt

1 cup sugar

2 cups frozen or fresh blueberries

TIP: Another option for powdered egg replacer is xantham gum powder, which is available at most natural food stores. Add 1½ teaspoons for this recipe.

Preheat the oven to 350°F. Lightly oil muffin tins.

In a large bowl, combine the flour, baking powder and salt. In a second bowl, combine the egg replacer, corn oil and yogurt. Whisk in the sugar until creamed, about 2 minutes.

Add the blueberries to the dry ingredients and mix to disperse evenly. Add the wet mixture and stir only until just combined.

Scoop 3–4 tablespoons of batter into each muffin cup. Bake 25–30 minutes or until the top edges of the muffins just begin to brown.

Remove the muffins from the oven and let cool 5 minutes before removing them from the tins. The muffins keep several days stored in an airtight container.

sticky cinnamon buns

Nothing beats hot cinnamon rolls on a blustery, cold morning. Settle in with a cup of tea, a thick newspaper and one of these fresh from the oven.

To save time in the morning, start the rolls the night before. Prepare them to the point just before the final rising, then refrigerate overnight. They also can be frozen at this stage up to 2 months.

DOUGH:

2½ cups water

4 cups unbleached white flour

½ cup maple syrup

1½ tablespoons yeast

3½ cups whole wheat pastry flour

1¼ teaspoons sea salt

1 teaspoon cinnamon

1½ cups water

½ cup corn oil

SYRUP MIXTURE:

1 cup barley malt syrup or molasses

½ cup maple syrup

¼ cup corn oil

1 tablespoon vanilla

2 teaspoons cinnamon

FILLING:

1 cup raisins *or* dried cranberries *or* apricots *or* a combination

1 cup roasted walnuts, chopped

For the dough, pour 1 cup of water into a small saucepan and heat over a low flame until just lukewarm. Transfer the water to a small bowl and add ½ cup white flour and the maple syrup. Mix well, then sprinkle the yeast into the mixture. Mix and set aside 10 minutes to activate yeast.

In another bowl, combine the remaining unbleached white flour, whole wheat pastry flour, salt and cinnamon.

In a third large bowl, combine the remaining water and ½ cup corn oil. Add the yeast mixture and stir to combine.

Slowly stir the dry ingredients into the wet ingredients. Knead about 10 minutes or until the dough is elastic and smooth. Cover with a damp dish towel and set aside in a warm, draft-free area to rise 1 hour. Dough should double in size.

While the dough rises, whisk together all the ingredients for the syrup in a medium bowl. Set aside.

Once the dough has doubled, transfer to a dry, lightly floured surface. Roll out into a long rectangle, about the size of a baking sheet. Spread about ⅔ of the syrup mixture over the dough. Sprinkle the raisins and nuts over the syrup.

Starting from the short side, roll the dough "jelly roll style" into a thick log. With a serrated knife, slice the log into rounds about 1¼ inches thick.

Place the slices, cut sides up, on a parchment paper-lined baking sheet. The rounds should just barely touch each other. Leave a 2-inch space around the outer edges of the pan.

Preheat the oven to 350°F.

Cover the rolls lightly with plastic wrap and let rise another 30 minutes. Remove the plastic wrap and bake 15 minutes. Remove from the oven and brush with the remaining syrup mixture. Bake another 10 minutes or until puffed and lightly golden.

cranberry-almond pancakes

This luscious pancake bursts with flavor. Serve with maple syrup on a chilly morning, or as a light Sunday supper.

START TO FINISH:

20 minutes

Makes 2 servings

TIP: It can be hard to find cranberries after Christmas. Buy several extra bags when they are in season and store them in the freezer. They should keep through summer.

To test the temperature of the skillet, sprinkle a few drops of water in it. If they bubble, the pan is hot enough to make pancakes.

1 cup unbleached white flour

1 teaspoon baking soda

1 teaspoon baking powder

1 cup vanilla soy milk

1 tablespoon brown rice syrup *or* maple syrup

1 tablespoon plus 1 teaspoon corn oil

½ teaspoon salt

3 tablespoons fresh or frozen cranberries

2 tablespoons almond slivers

In a large bowl, combine flour, baking powder and baking soda. Add soy milk, brown rice syrup, 1 tablespoon corn oil and salt and whisk until well blended. Fold in cranberries and almonds.

Heat remaining oil in a medium skillet over a medium flame. Pour about ¼ cup of the batter into the skillet and rotate the pan to evenly distribute. Cook until bubbles form around the edges of the pancake, about 3 minutes.

Flip the pancake and cook another 1–2 minutes. Repeat with remaining batter.

french toast

Give this a try the next time you want to linger over the Sunday paper and enjoy an out-of-the-ordinary breakfast. These toasts get wonderfully crispy.

    2 bananas
    1 cup vanilla soy yogurt
    1 teaspoon nutritional yeast flakes
    ½ teaspoon cinnamon
       Pinch nutmeg, freshly grated
  4–6 slices bread, 1½ inches thick
    1 cup frozen blueberries
    ½ cup maple syrup

Preheat the oven to 425°F. Liberally oil a large baking sheet.

Combine bananas, yogurt, yeast flakes, cinnamon and nutmeg in a food processor or blender. Process until quite smooth. Transfer to a shallow bowl.

Dip bread into the banana mixture, turning to coat both sides.

Arrange the slices in a single layer on the prepared baking sheet. Bake about 10–12 minutes, then flip slices and bake another 5 minutes.

While the toast bakes, combine the maple syrup and blueberries in a small saucepan. Simmer 3 minutes.

To serve, spoon syrup mixture over slices of toast.

START TO FINISH:
20 minutes
Makes 2–3 servings

TIP: Add variety by varying the bread type. Try sourdough, cinnamon raisin, cranberry nut, etc. We've used a cherry pecan that is fantastic.

Be sure to use a thin (usually inexpensive) baking sheet. Thicker ones designed to prevent burning also prevent the browning so important for good toast.

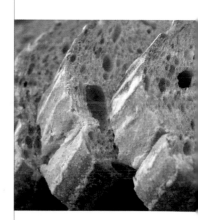

breakfast fruit smoothie

A heavy breakfast can weigh you down, especially if you hit the gym before heading to work. Try a thick, fruity smoothie instead for a filling but light start.

1 **frozen banana**
½ **cup frozen berries**
   Scant pinch sea salt
½ **teaspoon lemon juice**
6 **ounces soft, silken tofu or 1 scoop soy protein powder**
¾ **cup vanilla soy or rice milk**

Combine all ingredients in a blender. Process until smooth, about 30 seconds to 1 minute.

NOTE: Though fresh fruit is great in smoothies, we prefer frozen. This gives the drink a thicker, more satisfying body. We especially like frozen bananas, which we peel and freeze in storage bags.

For the berries, blueberries and strawberries are best. Raspberries taste great, but the seeds bother some people.

The salt and lemon juice play an important role in heightening the other flavors.

glossary

Most of these ingredients are available in the ethnic sections of large grocers or at natural food stores.

Agar (AY-gar): A sea vegetable-based thickener used in desserts and jellies. A vegan alternative to gelatin.

Arame (AIR-ah-may): A sweet sea vegetable used in grain and pasta dishes. The thin, black strands are sold dry and double in volume when soaked in water.

Arborio rice: An Italian short-grain rice with a high starch content. Used in risotto.

Arrowroot: An alternative to cornstarch that is used as a thickener for sauces, desserts and soups. It also can be used as a binder in egg-free baking.

Basmati rice: A fragrant, long-grain rice used in curries.

Bean thread noodles: These noodles resemble brittle fishing line. Prepare by soaking for several minutes in warm water. Also called glass or cellophane noodles.

Black mustard seeds: More pungent than yellow mustard seeds, these seeds are a common ingredient in Indian cooking.

Brown rice syrup: A thick sweetener made from rice. It resembles maple syrup but has a more delicate sweetness.

Bulgur: A quick-cooking, parboiled wheat kernel similar in appearance to couscous. Common in tabouli, pilafs and soups.

Candied ginger: Chunks of fresh ginger steeped in a water and sugar solution and dried. Also called crystallized ginger.

Capers: Edible buds of a Mediterranean shrub, most often used in antipasto, salads and dips.

Cashew butter: A peanut butter-like spread made from cashew nuts.

Couscous: A quick-cooking granular pasta made from semolina flour, water and salt. Commonly mixed with vegetables or tossed into salads. Also available in whole wheat varieties.

Curry paste: A paste made from spices, garlic and other seasonings. Used in curries and other Indian and Asian dishes. Available commercially in a variety of flavors, including Thai red.

Egg replacer: A powdered vegan substitute for eggs. Used in baking. Made from a variety of starches, including potato flour.

Extra-virgin olive oil: The highest quality, purest and most flavorful olive oil variety. Heat diminishes the flavor. Use light olive oil for high-heat cooking.

Fava beans (FAH-vuh): Available dried, canned and sometimes fresh. Fava beans have a tough skin that should be removed by blanching prior to cooking. Popular in Mediterranean and Middle Eastern dishes. Also called broad beans.

Flax seeds: Small, brown, nutrient-dense seeds. Used whole or ground to add a nutty flavor to baked goods.

Galangal: Similar to ginger but with a deeper, more savory flavor. Powdered ginger can be substituted.

Garam masala: A spice mixture made from chili peppers, cardamom, mustard and coriander seeds.

Hiziki (Hee-ZJI-kee): A sea vegetable similar to arame but with a stronger flavor and more robust strands.

Kombu (KOM-boo): A sea vegetable used to flavor soups and sauces. Sold in large, wide strips. Often removed from the dish and discarded before serving.

Kuzu (KOO-zoo): A natural thickening agent that resembles cornstarch but with clumps. Used to thicken soups, puddings and gravies. Also called kudzu.

Lemon grass: An aromatic herb with a pungent flavor used in Vietnamese and Thai cooking. Available fresh, dried or powdered.

Maple syrup crystals: Maple syrup that has been dried and broken into granules.

Matzo meal: A flour made from matzo bread, the Jewish flatbread.

Mirin (MEER-in): A Japanese rice cooking wine with a sweet, mild flavor. Avoid brands with added sugar; it usually indicates lower quality.

Miso (MEE-so): A paste made from fermented soybeans. Available in a variety of flavors. Generally, light misos are sweet and dark misos are savory.

Natural shortening: Unlike conventional shortenings, which are made from unhealthy hydrogenated oils, natural shortenings use tropical oils, which are solid at room temperature.

Nori: A sea vegetable that has been pressed into sheets. Used to make sushi.

Nutritional yeast flakes: An inactive yeast available as flakes or powder. Has a salty cheese-like flavor.

Pesto: An Italian sauce traditionally made from olive oil, basil, garlic and pine nuts. Used on pasta, pizza and crostini.

Pine nuts: The edible seeds from the pine cones of the piñon tree (a variety of pine tree). Also called pignoli.

Plantains: The starchy fruit of a variety of banana plant. Must be cooked.

Rice milk: A nondairy milk made from rice. A good substitute for dairy milk, especially in baking and puddings. Available in a variety of flavors.

Rice paper wrappers: Brittle translucent sheets made from rice flour and used in fresh and fried spring rolls. The wrappers are softened by soaking briefly in warm water.

Rice vinegar: A mild vinegar made from fermented brown rice. Used in Asian cooking. Available in seasoned and unseasoned varieties.

Sea salt: Contains no additives or colorings and is not processed with high heat, as table salt is. A higher mineral content also lends a deeper flavor.

Seitan: A meat substitute made from wheat gluten.

Soba noodles: An Asian noodle made from buckwheat flour. High in protein.

Soy milk: A nondairy milk substitute made from soybeans. A good substitute for dairy milk, especially in baking and puddings. Available in a variety of flavors.

Sushi rice: A short-grain rice that cooks up sticky. Usually flavored with rice vinegar before being used in sushi.

Tahini: A peanut butter-like spread made from sesame seeds. Used in hummus, sauces, dips and dressings.

Tamari: A soy sauce that contains no wheat and often is lower in sodium than traditional varieties.

Tamarind concentrate: A paste made from fruit native to Asia and northern Africa. Popular in Indian and Thai food.

Tempeh: A meat substitute made from fermented soybeans. Raw tempeh has a bitter taste but develops a mild nutty flavor when cooked.

Toasted sesame seed oil: A nutty, savory oil great for sautéing and sprinkling over cooked vegetables. Common in Asian cooking.

Tofu: Soybean curd available in a variety of textures and flavors. Silken tofu is best for sauces and puddings. Firm tofu is best marinated and baked or grilled.

Turmeric: An East Indian plant that's related to the ginger family. Used extensively in Indian cooking.

Udon noodles: A thin, chewy Asian noodle made from whole wheat flour.

Umeboshi plums: A pickled Asian plum used to season soups, grains, sauces and vegetables.

Umeboshi vinegar: A salty liquid similar to vinegar. Used to season steamed vegetables and dressings.

Wasabi powder: A horseradish-like seasoning available as a powder or paste. Used as a condiment for sushi. Also can be added to mashed potatoes and other vegetables to add heat.

sources

Rarely do recipes originate with single sources. They are an aggregate of input from the many hands and mouths that enjoyed them over the years.

Many also begin as the recipes of others but morph as they are repeated, tinkered with and passed along over the years.

It would be impossible to acknowledge all the hands, mouths and sources that have influenced us, but their inspiration and wisdom are appreciated and respected.

However, we can pay heed to many of the well-written cookbooks and publications that served as invaluable references.

Anderson, Jean, *The Food of Portugal*, William Morrow

Atlas, Nava, and Kayte, Lillian, *Vegetarian Express*, Little Brown

Barnard, Tanya, and Kramer, Sarah, *The Garden of Vegan*, Arsenal Pulp Press

Barnard, Tanya, and Kramer, Sarah, *How It All Vegan*, Arsenal Pulp Press

Berley, Peter, *The Modern Vegetarian Kitchen*, Regan Books

Caldicott, Chris and Carolyn, *The Spice Routes*, Soma Books

Caldicott, Chris and Carolyn, *World Food Café*, Soma Books

Christensen, Sally J., and Piper de Vries, Frances, eds., *Weimar Institute's Newstart Lifestyle Cookbook*, Thomas Nelson Publishers

Cook's Illustrated, *The Best Recipe*, America's Test Kitchen

Cook's Illustrated magazine, America's Test Kitchen

Freed, Hermine, *The Vegan Epicure*, Sterling Publishing

Geiskopf-Hadler, Susann, and Toomay, Mindy, *The Vegan Gourmet*, Prima Publishing

Gordon, Arthur, *The Irregardless Cooks*, Ten Speed Press

Jackson, Ann, *Heart of the Home*

Jaffrey, Madhur, *Madhur Jaffrey's World Vegetarian*, Clarkson Potter

Johns, Pamela Sheldon, *Pasta!*, Ten Speed Press

Katzen, Mollie, *Moosewood Cookbook*, Ten Speed Press

Klein, Donna, *The Mediterranean Vegan Kitchen*, HP Books

Kornfeld, Myra, and Minot, George, *The Voluptuous Vegan*, Clarkson Potter

La Place, Viana, and Kleiman, Evan, *Cucina Rustica*, William Morrow

Lukins, Sheila, *All Around the World Cookbook*, Workman Publishing

Mair, Nancy, *The Intimate Vegetarian*, Renaissance Books

McCarty, Meredith, *Fresh from a Vegetarian Kitchen*, St. Martin's Press

McCarty, Meredith, *Sweet and Natural*, St. Martin's Press

McEachern, Leslie, *The Angelica Home Kitchen*, Ten Speed Press

Natural Health magazine, Weider Publications

Nazzaro, Lorel, *The Pesto Manifesto*, Chelsea Green Publishing

Pirello, Christina, *Cooking the Whole Foods Way*, HP Books

Raichlen, Steven, *Healthy Jewish Cooking*, Viking

Robertson, Laurel; Flinders, Carol; and Ruppenthal, Brian, *The New Laurel's Kitchen*, Ten Speed Press

Rosso, Julee, *Great Good Food*, Crown Publishers

Schechter, Doris, *My Most Favorite Dessert Company Cookbook*, Harper Collins

Schneider, Elizabeth, *Vegetables from Amaranth to Zucchini*, William Morrow

Scicolone, Michele, *Italian Holiday Cooking*, William Morrow

Stepaniak, Joanne, *The Uncheese Cookbook*, Book Publishing Company

Tucker, Eric, and Westerdahl, John, *The Millennium Cookbook*, Ten Speed Press

Vegetarian Times magazine, Sabot Publishing

Veggie Life magazine, EGW Publishing

Wells, Troth, *Global Vegetarian Cooking*, Interlink Books

index